This book is dedicated to the life and work of Rich Roat: A friend, collaborator, and creative hero.

BRINGING BACK *MST3K*: THE MAKING OF
"THE RETURN" & "THE GAUNTLET"
ISBN: 9780578526270
Published by Askwith&Co SSD.
Kickstarter Edition: August 2019.
© 2019 Satellite of Love LLC

Bringing Back
MST3K

The Making of *The Return* & *The Gauntlet*

by Joel Hodgson, Ivan Askwith &
The Alternaversal Vision Team

Contents

Dear MST3K Revival League,

Joel here, with one more update for you… and this is a big one. If you're reading this, it means you're now holding the *final reward* from both our #BringBackMST3K Kickstarter and the *MST3K* Season 12 Pledge Drive: our official "behind the scenes" coffee table book.

And you know, even though it's been a long time coming, I hope you'll agree it was worth the wait. In the end, I'm glad it took us a while to finish this book, because it's also given us some time to reflect on everything that's happened over the last few years.

Anyway, I guess you can kind of think of this book as the longest "Backer Update" I'll ever write: over 100 pages of new material, most of which has never been shared before. And, the last time I checked, this book also included over 80 pages of text and more than 500 hand-picked illustrations and photos.

One of the biggest challenges – and one of the reasons our team has taken more than two years of work to finally finish this book – is that there are many ways to organize so much material. We tried lots of them, and created many different drafts of this book. But in the end, there was only one approach that really made sense for me, and that was to just go in order and show you how the process works, from start to finish. So, that's what we did.

In the song "Trust Us", by Captain Beefheart and His Magic Band, there's a really wonderful line where he says:

"You gotta see before you see."

I've thought about that lyric a lot over the last few years, both as our team worked to prepare two new seasons of *Mystery Science Theater,* and also as we tried to find the best way to share that experience with all of you. And I guess what I like about it, is that it poses a riddle to anyone who wants to make something new, or see something new:

How **can you see something before you see it?**

C.B. makes a few suggestions with his lyrics:

You gotta hear without fear, oh /
You gotta feel to reveal /
You gotta touch without taint /
Such is is and uh ain't is ain't

I think he may have been kidding on that last line, but the rest of the verses – if you let them – start to feel like a couple of those Zen koans from *The Collection of Stone and Sand.*

So yeah, I guess the question this book is really trying to answer is, "How do you see the new version of *MST3K* before you see it?"

Because, you know, that's what we had to do.

In the pages that follow, we've tried to give you a really detailed look at the method that allowed us to *see it*, piece by piece, until we could ultimately show it to you.

Also, I realize that movie riffing is the creative art form that really got us to the dance, but I've gotta tell you: riffs themselves aren't all that photogenic, or fun to look at. So, this is a visual document that covers just about everything *except* the writing process.

Anyway, now that you know what I wanted to do with this book, here's how it all works. We've organized everything into three important stages:

1. **CONCEPTING**, where we come up with a vision, and all of the ideas;
2. **BUILDING,** where the entire team works to make that vision possible; *and*
3. **SHOOTING,** where everything we've created is captured on screen.

Also, since the book took so much longer than we expected to complete, we've added in a whole section that follows the entire process *again* for Season 12.

And then, I wanted to take a few pages to give credit to a lot of the wonderful, talented collaborators who worked behind-the-scenes to create everything you'll see in this book. I also wanted to take one last chance to thank the people who made this whole thing possible. (That's you!)

So yeah, that's what you'll find in this book. I'm pretty pleased with how it came out, and all of the stories and details it gave us the chance to share with you.

But you know, since this book is called "Bringing Back *MST3K*", I want to take a few pages to start by talking about *how* we were able to bring the show back.

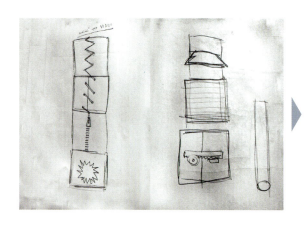

1987
CONCEPT SKETCHES

1988
KTMA PILOT

1988-1989
KTMA SERIES

1989-1996
COMEDY CHANNEL /
COMEDY CENTRAL

THE FIRST RIFF
The bottom picture shows our very first movie riff –
"That's no meteor! That's a battle station!" – from the
KTMA pilot, featuring *The Green Slime*. While we lost
the rights to use this film for the series, we included
the riff in an ad to promote the show before it pre-
miered on Thanksgiving Day in 1988.

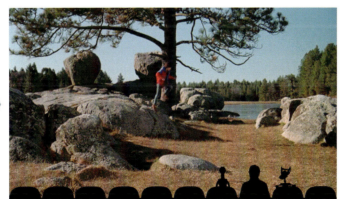

1997-1999
THE SCI-FI CHANNEL

2017–Present
NETFLIX

THE MORE THINGS CHANGE...
The sets and bots have undergone improvements
over the years. The movies? Not so much.

The Evolution of *MST3K*

As most of you know, *Mystery Science Theater* first debuted over thirty years ago, as a UHF access show on KTMA TV 23, in Minneapolis and St. Paul, Minnesota.

But as I looked through all of the art and photos from the making of *The Return* and *The Gauntlet*, I've come to realize that the process for making the new *MST3K* was actually pretty similar to making the original KTMA pilot.

In both cases, the process started with drawings in my notebook (Column 1), which helped me explain the idea to the crew, writers and producers who would work on the show – first at KTMA, in 1988 (Column 2), and again for the new series, in 2016 (Column 6).

As you can see, these original ideas remain to this day: host segments, the doorway sequence, and silhouettes in the movie theater. Through the rest of this book, I'll tell you more about how these ideas evolved, but when you look at all of these stages together, you can start to understand some of the biggest questions we needed to answer for *The Return*:

• *How much should each of these core elements evolve?*

• *What new elements would we need to add, to bring* MST3K *back to life in a way that felt fresh, yet familiar?*

Or, to put it another way, we really had to ask:

"What makes *Mystery Science Theater 3000*, *Mystery Science Theater 3000*?"

But before we could really answer that, we had to answer a more pressing question: after all, the last new episode of *MST* had aired in August of 1999.

I had known for years that I wanted to make new episodes of *Mystery Science Theater*. The question I still had to answer, of course, was *how*.

Bring Back MYSTERY SCIENCE THEATER 3000

by **Joel Hodgson**

114% FUNDED!

$600,000 RAISED OUTSIDE OF KICKSTARTER!

| EPISODES 1-3 UNLOCKED! $2,000,000 | EPISODES 4-6 UNLOCKED! $3,300,000 | EPISODES 7-9 UNLOCKED! $4,400,000 | EPISODES 10-12 UNLOCKED! $5,500,000 | EPISODES 13-14 UNLOCKED! $6,300,000 |

📍 Minneapolis, MN   🏷 Television

48,270
backers

$5,764,229
pledged of $2,000,000 goal

0
days to go

Back This Project

⭐ Remind me

This project will only be funded if at least $2,000,000 is pledged by Sat, Dec 12 2015 1:00 AM EST.

Help #BringBackMST3K, one of the most beloved cult television series ever, for a new season of up to 12 feature-length episodes!

Joel Hodgson

🌐 First created |
👤 1 backed
📍 joelhodgson.com

See full bio   Contact me

Pledge US$ 10 or more

EXPERIMENT 010: JUST HELPING

Don't need a lot of fancy rewards? Don't have a lot to give? That's okay, friend. Come on in here, under the big tent, and join the club!

You'll get EXCLUSIVE INFO UPDATES, chock-full of behind-the-scenes access, sketches, videos, set reports and more.

Plus, you can prove you helped with a PRINTABLE "MST3K INFORMATION CLUB 2" MEMBERSHIP CERTIFICATE AND ID CARD.

ESTIMATED DELIVERY
Mar 2016

5,319 backers

Pledge US$ 25 or more

EXPERIMENT 025: WE'VE GOT MOVIE SIGN!

THE FINAL COUNTDOWN IS HERE.

Our Kickstarter ENDS TONIGHT at 10 PM PST.

We've raised *almost* enough to make a full TWELVE EPISODES, but it's gonna be close... so we're pulling out all the stops!

DOUBLE FEATURE COUNTDOWN
CONCLUDES TODAY, STARTING AT 2 PM PST
Each day this week, we've livestreamed a new MST3K Double Feature: two of Joel's favorite episodes back-to-back, with new introductions & fan mail!

LIVE COUNTDOWN TELETHON
w/ JOEL & FRIENDS
LIVESTREAM POWERED BY X〔SN〕

STARTS TONIGHT @ 5 PM PST

Spend the FINAL 5 HOURS live online with Joel, our next cast & special guests!
We'll have comedy, music, magic, games, special offers and more.

Bringing Back *MST3K*

The answer to that question didn't become clear until mid-2013, when I heard that fans of a cancelled television show called *Veronica Mars* had used a new platform called Kickstarter to bring the show back as a movie. It seemed like an amazing way to "save" shows like *Mystery Science Theater* – things that fans wanted, but that studios and networks didn't really "get."

But, even though I would wonder about doing a Kickstarter sometimes, I never really took the idea seriously until I had a meal with Harold Buchholz. Harold first approached me to talk about adapting *Cinematic Titanic* – another riffing group I was performing with – as a comic book, but once we started talking about that, we became even more interested in figuring out how to get the rights we'd need to make more *MST*.

Harold was the first person who convinced me that we might really be able to bring the show back through a Kickstarter campaign, and he seemed organized enough to help me realize that idea. From there, the next step was to partner with Shout! Factory, who helped us secure the rights we needed, and our amazing crowdfunding strategist and producer, Ivan Askwith.

I had first heard about Ivan through a mutual friend, the magician Derek Delgaudio, who told me that Ivan had run the *Veronica Mars* Kickstarter, as well as multi-million dollar campaigns for *Reading Rainbow* and *Super Troopers 2*, and that he specialized in working with fans to get things made outside of traditional channels. So, it seemed like a good idea to meet with him.

Since then, Ivan has been an important force in bringing back *Mystery Science Theater 3000*, responsible not just for planning and running the Kickstarter, but also for working with me on backer updates, managing the design and creation of all of our rewards, planning our premieres, hosting set visits for fans, and producing both *The Return* and *The Gauntlet*. He also took the lead on curating the subject matter for this book, and helped me step back and organize all of this material.

MAKING THE PITCH
The shoot for our Kickstarter videos was very elaborate. It was also the first time that Jonah, Felicia, Hampton and Baron appeared in their new *Mystery Science* roles.

PASSING THE BATON (LEFT)
At far left, the first picture Jonah took with me, on the day of our Kickstarter shoot.

TRACKING PROGRESS (CENTER)
Watching the Kickstarter page just moments after launch, and waiting for the first pledges to show up on the counter. It was a long month.

TRACKING PROGRESS (RIGHT)
A photo sent to backers not long after we passed our first major milestone of $1 million.

TURKEY DAY 2015
Our friends at Kickstarter let us take over their Brooklyn headquarters to shoot an elaborate series of sketches for the Turkey Day Marathon, which doubled as a fundraiser.

Over the month of our Kickstarter, we worked pretty much around the clock: writing updates, making announcements, adding new rewards, hosting livestream Q&A sessions and screenings of old episodes, and recruiting some of *MST*'s famous friends to help spread the word.

All of this led to our big finale on December 11, 2015, when we broadcast our "Final Countdown," a five-hour online telethon to wrap up our Kickstarter live from the floor of Meltdown Comics in LA.

To tell you the truth, I wasn't sure about it. We were all pretty tired by that point, and it seemed like a lot could go wrong. But, Ivan reminded me that it was important to spend the final night of the Kickstarter with all of you.

And you know, even though a lot of things *did* go wrong – in true *Mystery Science* fashion – we had a great time, and it really helped us across the finish line. In the end, it was a very memorable night. Our wonderful friends, producers and

songwriters Paul and Storm hosted, and Felicia and Patton both stopped in for a visit. Felicia charmed the crowd, and Patton used his signature sense of humor to keep everyone laughing… even when we ran into "technical difficulties."

Many of our talented friends also joined us on camera to help keep the night interesting, including comedians Kate Micucci, Dana Snyder, and Dana Gould (as William Shatner as Dr. Zaius); magicians John Carney and Rob Zabreckie;

YouTube riffing celebrities *Game Grumps* (who riffed a video game version of *Manos* with Crow); and many more.

And, we also shared video messages and last-minute special rewards from friends including vlogger Hank Green, EGOT-winner Bobby Lopez, magicians Penn & Teller, artist Pen Ward, musicians Freezepop and Jonathan Coulton, writer John Hodgman, and *Rick & Morty*'s Dan Harmon and Justin Roiland.

KEEP CIRCULATING THE URL.

BringBackMST3K.com
#BringBackMST3K

The rest, of course, you know. In the final hours of the Kickstarter, we passed our final funding goal of $5.5 million, and then kept going, raising an astonishing final total of *$6.3 million*: enough to shoot fourteen new episodes! (That's two more than even *we* had hoped for.)

It also meant that we passed *Veronica Mars* to become the most-funded film or television crowdfunding campaign ever, a title we were proud to hold for over *three years*, until we finally passed it along to our friends at *Critical Role* in April 2019.

But, you know, the end of the Kickstarter was really just the *beginning* of the journey to #BringBackMST3K.

Since then, we've produced 20 new episodes across two seasons of *Mystery Science Theater 3000* on Netflix, written and published an *MST* comic book with our friends at Dark Horse, and visited with thousands of you during two national live tours. And, of course, we're still hard at work planning what comes next.

Anyway, that's for another day. For now, I want to share everything I can about our creative process, and show you some of the amazing work that went into bringing back *Mystery Science Theater 3000*.

Also, you know that song I was talking about? Well, I think I might have an answer to the riddle. *How can you see something before you can see it?* Captain Beefheart, in his wisdom, buried the lead in the title of the song:

"Trust Us."

How did this all happen? You trusted us… and I can't thank you enough.

Cheers & Thanks,

Joel Hodgson

PHASE ONE

Concepting

The first important step is **CONCEPTING.**

In this stage, you really start by focus on imagining the world: how it feels, what the tone should be like, and how it all needs to work.

Because, you know, you can't start building *anything* until you know what you want to make!

And actually, for the return of *Mystery Science Theater 3000,* the first ideas and concepts started to form a few years *before* we launched the Kickstarter. At first, I was just playing around, imagining what an "updated" version of *Mystery Science Theater* might feel like.

So yeah, in this first section, you'll see a lot of notes and little sketches – and as you go through these pages, you'll get a chance to see how much the artwork changes and improves as we really get into the process, and a lot of very talented people get involved.

We started with my **ROUGH SKETCHES** (P.14) and some experiments with **3-D COLLAGE & MAQUETTES** (P.16), and then worked on a handful of very early **SCRIPTS & STORYBOARDS** (P.18), just to help us figure out the scope of the whole thing, and how big we wanted it to feel. Once these first parts of development are done, it's much easier to bring people onto the team.

Then, with the help of some amazing visual artists, we moved into **INSPIRATIONAL ART** (P.20),

which is where you don't worry too much about how you'll bring the ideas to life, but really try to capture the mood and tone you're hoping for. That's really critical, because it lets everyone on the team start imagining the same thing before you start getting too specific.

Once we all know what we're aiming for, the next step is to draw up **CONCEPT ART** (P.26), which is where the illustrations start to get a lot more anchored in the real world, and to suggest how the ideas we're imagining could actually be created on screen. When you work with great concept artists, you also start to make real decisions about how the show will take shape.

And then, as I'll show you, you assemble all of this amazing work that everyone has done into detailed **PRODUCTION STORYBOARDS** (P.38), so that you have a real plan for what to start building, and how you'll be using it in the final show.

So yeah, those are the steps involved in CONCEPTING... but it'll probably help more if I just *show* you what I'm talking about, huh?

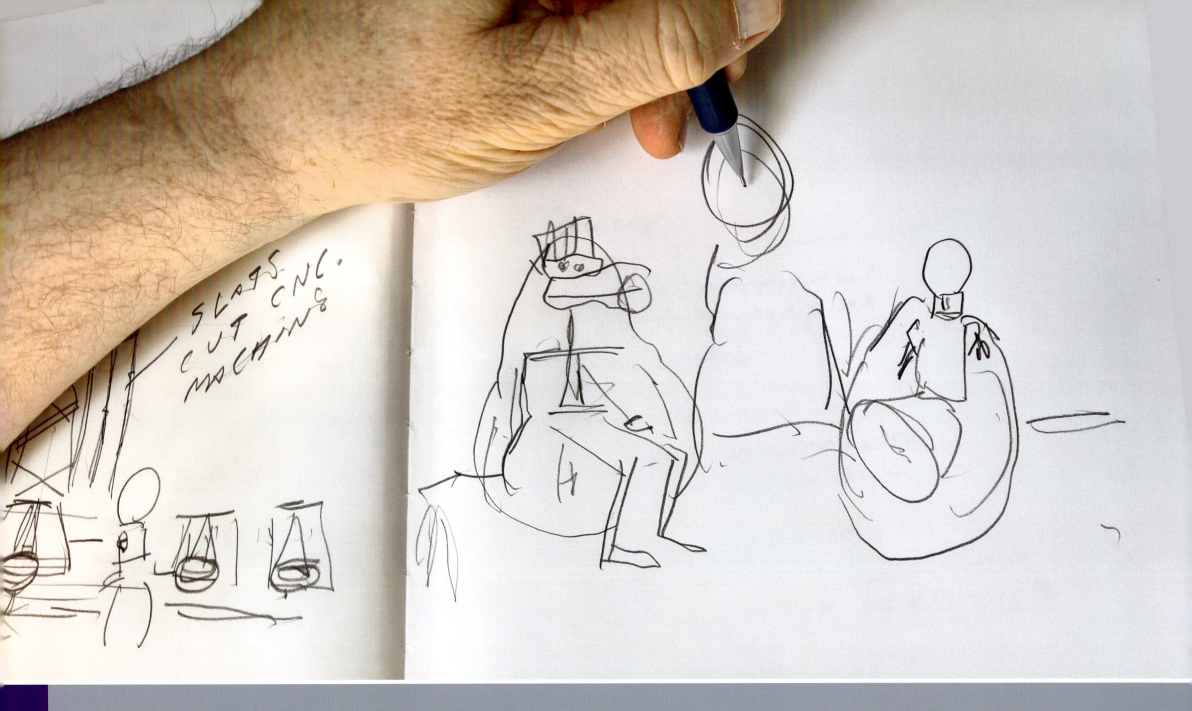

SLATS
CUT CNC.
MACHINE

Rough Sketches

The first steps in creating the new *Mystery Science Theater* mostly started, as I said, with sketches in my notebooks. For me, my notebooks are kind of a way to "bank" ideas, even if I'm not sure which ones I'll want to use.

So yeah, it all starts with lots of drawings and notes. I've actually been doing sketches like these since my freshman year in college, when I was designing sculptures, puppets and props for my comedy magic shows. I've found that once I draw the right sketch and feel like I have the idea "banked," I'm able to move on.

Anyway, for a period of about seven years before we launched the Kickstarter, I spent a lot of time trying to collect enough new ideas to feel like *The Return* could be a novel, cohesive world that would adapt to a new cast and new writers, but also still "feel" like *MST*, and be realized using the same production methods we had always used.

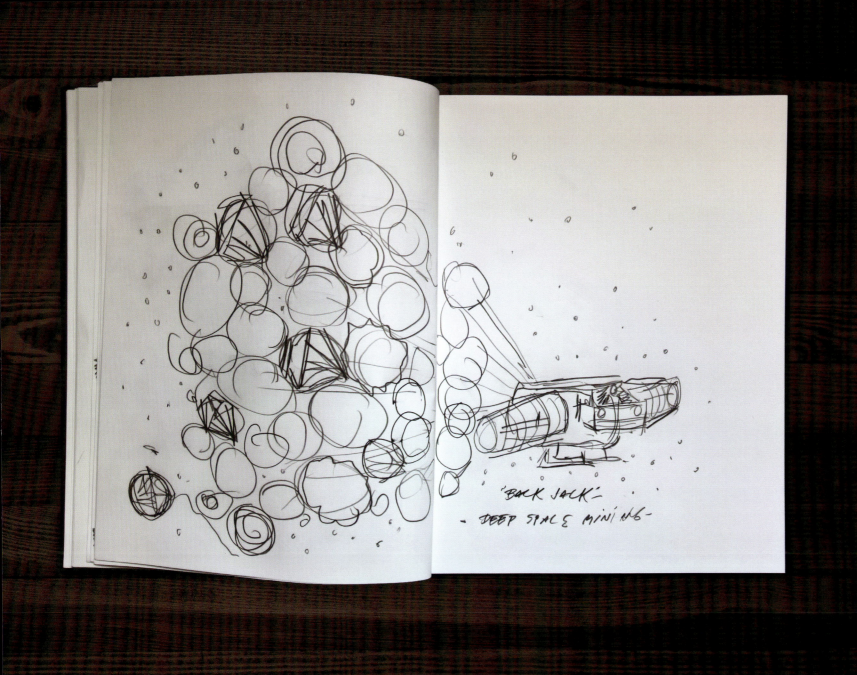

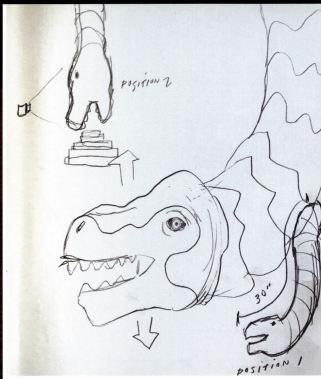

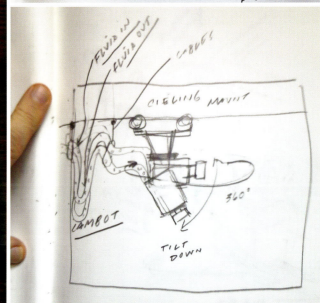

- **BOTS IN BEAN BAGS (P.14)**
An early sketch of the Bots in their bean bag chairs. I know what you're thinking, and yes: even as a pencil sketch, seeing Crow's legs is a little unnerving. Also, even when I drew this first sketch, I was already trying to imagine how we'd run the control sticks through the beanbags and behind the desk, so the puppeteers could control Crow and Servo.

(And yes, someone's a lefty.)

- **BACKJACK & PAYLOAD (LEFT)**
When you first have an idea, it's not always arranged spatially, so you need to figure out what you're drawing, and how it exists in real space. Sometimes, an idea that works in your head doesn't really work on paper. Sketches help you figure out things like scale, proportions, and possible mechanical issues. Here, I knew that the Backjack should be much smaller than the payload it's hauling.

- **REPTILICUS METALLICUS (TOP RIGHT)**
The idea of having Reptilicus "eat" the host came to me very early – even before I knew who the host would be! But in the sketch, you can see I was already thinking about where the camera would be placed.

- **CAMBOT (BOTTOM RIGHT)**
Cambot goes fluid by tapping into Kingachrome – which meant we needed to figure out how Cambot would be mounted to the ceiling, but still capture all the shots we need. (And yes, "going fluid" *was* just as messy as it sounds.)

EARLY DEVELOPMENT

3-D Collage & Maquettes

Even though there's a lot you can figure out in a sketch, I also like thinking through 3-D models. Once you have a model of something, it makes an idea feel like it's actually beginning to come into the world, you know?

This might be a good time to explain that I probably have *pareidolia*, which is a psychological phenomenon that causes people to see patterns in random visuals. For me, I've always seen faces when I look at things, and that's probably how I get the idea to put a lot of common objects together to make new characters. This is similar to the method I used to make the original robots (Crow, Gypsy and Tom... who was originally called "Beeper").

If you look at the two robots above, you'll see that the first **M. WAVERLY** was actually inspired by a flower pot, action figure parts, a sand castle mold, and a foot pump that came with an air mattress. **GROWLER** was bashed together with parts from several action figures and other toys, pieces of vinyl tubing, and (I think) part of a bubble machine.

So yeah, early in the process, I started experimenting with some "3-D collages" to figure out some of the unique elements I was imagining for *The Return*, like a few new robot characters, a new "Moon 13" lair for the Mads, and Jonah's vehicle, the Backjack.

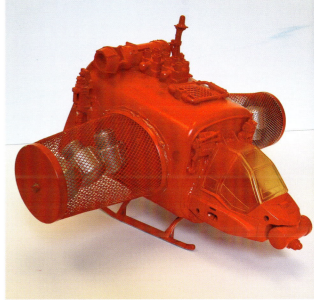

- **WAVERLY & GROWLER (P.16)**
  Thanks to 3-D scanning and printing, I was able to make all of the maquettes the same size, and then scale them up according to their personalities. That's also why these maquettes for Growler and M. Waverly are so beat up. (No, they haven't been playing paintball.) They were torn apart so we could 3-D scan their parts, then hot-glued back together to take reference photos.

- **MOONBASE 13 (TOP LEFT)**
  I learned a little trick from my brother, Jim, who is a long-time fabricator, art handler, and fine artist. To make the details really pop when you make a model, you use a coating of gunmetal gray paint. This technique also helps when building robots; once all the pieces are the same base color, it's easier to see the details clearly.

- **UNUSED MAQUETTES (BOTTOM)**
  I made a series of about 8-10 of these robot collages in the hopes that a couple of them would "speak" to me and give me that Geppetto moment I so crave. (I'm being semi-serious here. I remember looking at Crow when he was on my workbench prior to the KTMA pilot and I thought he looked pretty rad. Same with Gypsy and Servo.)

- **EARLY BACKJACK (RIGHT)**
  The Backjack was originally supposed to be a sort of space tugboat. I was interested in making the cockpit appear very small and claustrophobic, to help amplify the story of Jonah being isolated in space for so long. The name "Backjack" is a reference to the Steely Dan song, *Do It Again*. (You know: "Go back, Jack / Do it again.")

CONCEPTING

3001

Note; The Mads have orchestrated an elaborate live open to Mystery Science Theater that is actually a fiendish real time kidnapping in space set to music: it should have the timing and tension of a heist movie and also have the spirit of a amateur stage musical.

Story board note: the action is covered by three separate "cambots", (that are under the control of the Mads). The Cambots fly through space and do a sort of futuristic "three camera shoot" of the proceedings. We often see the cambots that are not shooting the scene flying into position for the next shot.

SPACE EXT. (CAMBOT 1#)

Cambot 1# is recording Cambot 2# and Cambot 3#. They are flying in a tight circle and rotating slowly in "Sync Lock" formation. On screen is a prompt that reads "Sync lock" and a counter counting down. We see stars in the distance slowly rotating panorama style

Note: This is the preshow position and the cambots will remain in this position indefinitely until they get the command to begin the show opening "sequence"

The prompt on screen finally counts down to 0 and the "sync lock" prompt disappears. Cambot 2# and Cambot 3# zoom off camera left as Cambot 1# drops down to show earth.

We see earth suspended in a star filled sky as several satellites drift on camera with the production company credits thematically embossed into their outer shells: Shout Factory, MST Studios, and Moon 13 limited. The first two satellites drift away leaving only the one labeled "Moon 13 limited". Then we see "TV's Frank" push on screen holding a dimensional metal set of words that reads "presentation" the letters, which are magnetized, attach to the satellite with a "click" as TV's Frank looks up at something approaching and jets off camera. Suddenly, the Satellite and "presents" sign is knocked from above by the metallic hull of a space ship cruising by. Cambot 1# pulls back to show that the hull belongs to the deep space salvage ship "The Tulsa". The spacecraft (from Gizmonic Institute) is hauling an array of valuable metallic ores from deep space.

CUT TO:

EXT SPACE EPIC SHOT (CAMBOT 3#)

We see a breathtaking master shot of the Tulsa moving through space toward the moon. Cambot 1# which is closer to the ship moves picture left and then goes off camera, it is being followed by TVS Frank who is flying via jetpack who also flies off camera.

CUT TO:

EXT SPACE MEDIUM (CAMBOT 1#)

The Tusla is about to cruise between two large meteors that are a drift, we see Cambot 2# and Cambot 3# in the upper left corner of the picture plane setting up for the coming reverse shots, as we catch a glimpse of TV's Frank ducking behind the meteor to the left and we also see a brief glimpse of Dr Clayton Forrester hiding behind the rock to right of the "tulsa".

CUT TO:

EXT SPACE (CAMBOT 2#)

the reverse shot of the space ship as it glides between the two meteors: from this perspective we see that TV's Frank and Dr. Clayton Forrester are hiding behind the large rocks, out of sight of the Tulsa and it's pilot. Both Forrest and Frank are each holding homemade devices, and as the ship passes the two jump from the rocks to jet along, next to the hull of the "Tulsa"

CUT TO:

EXT SPACE (CAMBOT 3#)

Medium shot of Doctor Forrester smiling at the camera as he attaches an old Victrola phonograph tricked out with big horseshoe magnets that attach to the hull of the "Tulsa" with a "click". Once attached, Forrester cranks the spring motor and the turntable begins rotating as Forrester sets the tone arm down on a hand pressed wax record labeled "Show open" written hastily in sharpie -- we hear an ominous hiphop jam that sounds a bit like "kiss kiss" by Chris Brown. Forester then pushes the Victrola's horn against the hull of the ship and then glides to the back of the ship.

CUT TO:

EXT. SPACE (CAMBOT 1#)

A medium shot of TVs Frank gliding next to the "Tulsa" with a device that is composed of large Hi-Fi reel to reel tape recorder that also fitted with big red horse-shoe magnets that attach to the hull of the ship with a "click" while, from behind it, TV's Frank pulls out a toilet plunger head attached to a hose that he presses against the side of "The Tulsa". He turns on the old reel to reel that lights up, obviously to record what's going on inside the ship. He then glides to the back of the ship and disappears behind it.

CUT TO:

EXT. SPACE (CAMBOT 2#)

tracking shot of the Tulsa as it now travels along the light side of the moon. Forrester and Frank are being towed behind while they hold the cable that are also towing the giant mineral samples.

SFX the music begins to swell dramatically as we see the moon surface pass into darkness, or, become the dark side of the moon.

CUT TO:

EXT "THE TULSA" THROUGH WINDSHIELD (CAMBOT 3#)

We see Bill: a tall, angular man, with boyish good looks, tapping his headset as he strains to make sense of the muffled sound of the musical jam coming through the hull. Next to Bill, in the co-pilot seat, is Rodney: a blue athletic looking and somewhat serious looking robot.

        BILL
    Gizmonic Institute? Can you hear me
    Ray?

        RADIO OPERATOR O.C.
    ...I'm looking at this mineral
    list: you landed one fantastic
    payload Bill - It's a treasure
    trove - we're going to be rich!

Bill smiles at the acknowledgement of his good fortune, but then, sees something in the distance far away.

EARLY DEVELOPMENT

Scripts & Storyboards

On most shows, I guess it's normal to start with a script, and then create storyboards to help you visualize it. But for me, the way I prefer to write a script is to *start* with lots of drawings and visual reference. I guess I do this so I feel familiar with the scope of where the production is going, and to help gauge costs before we get too far along.

(Truth be told, the reason I felt comfortable approaching Jim Mallon – and later, Don O'Connor – at KTMA about making *Mystery Science Theater 3000* there was because I was pretty certain it would be the least expensive comedy show on TV. But I digress.)

Once I started having a basic idea of what *MST3K: The Return* could be, I wrote a script for the brilliant storyboard artist, Andrew Dickman, who then set about realizing the ideas visually. That's what you're seeing here.

After he was done with those early storyboards, I was able to write a revised script that would work well on the page for those reading it, and I knew it made sense visually. People who write scripts and don't consider how the production will look are kind of hacks, if you're asking.

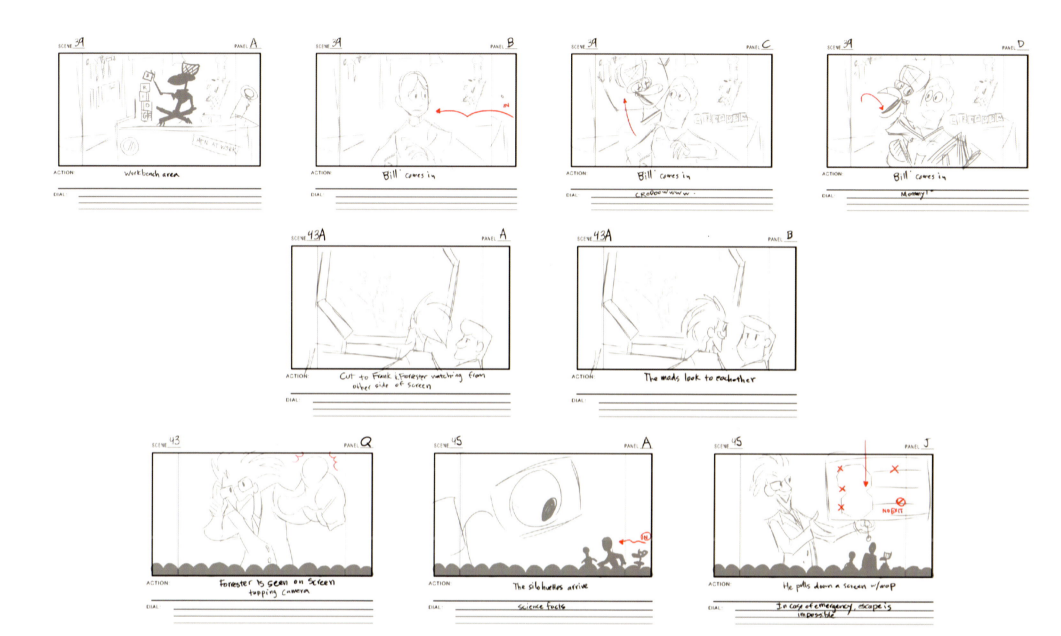

- **OPENING SCRIPT (P.18)**
  You'll notice from the heading on the first page of the script that I had been considering calling the new series *Mystery Science Theater 3001*.

- **PANELS 39A-39D (TOP ROW)**
  We were able to use a few of the ideas in the boards for the show open. These panels show Crow in silhouette, then he jumps on the host and rides "piggyback."

- **PANEL 43Q (BOTTOM LEFT)**
  As you can see, these boards were drawn when we thought the original Mads might return... but we were eventually able to use the idea of a Mad speaking directly to the host and Bots in our Kickstarter pitch video, when Kinga starts to scold Jonah and the Bots.

- **STORYBOARD CREDITS**
  A big, grateful thank you to the brilliant Andrew Dickman for making these original boards. It took almost *five years* before the project finally came to life, but these boards really helped lay the groundwork for what was to come.

INSPIRATIONAL ART
Gary Glover

Even though some ideas can be visualized with simple sketches and 3-D prototypes, a lot of the more elaborate or large-scale ideas really start with **inspirational art.**

The wonderful thing about great inspirational art is that, when you look at it, it almost feels like you can push your head through into the future and experience a moment from the show. When it really works, it's incredibly important, and helps inspire the direction for all of the other work we do.

Gary Glover, a long-time friend and early bot builder, has years of experience realizing ideas and illustrating them... so I was pleased that he was willing to lend us his deft skills to help imagine a few first flashes of the *MST3K* world that was to come.

(Gary was also kind enough to produce both inspirational art *and* on-screen production visuals for Season 12; check out P.87!)

- **SATELLITE OF LOVE (LEFT)**
  A really early illustration Gary used to help establish the mood and "alienation" vibe I imagined for the updated Satellite of Love.

- **JONAH & THE BOTS (RIGHT)**
  An early vision which included some nice ragtag details – such as the duct tape on Jonah's spacesuit, the drumsticks in his hands and punk rock boots – as well as the new iteration of Crow, showing his height and his more puppy-like feet and hands.

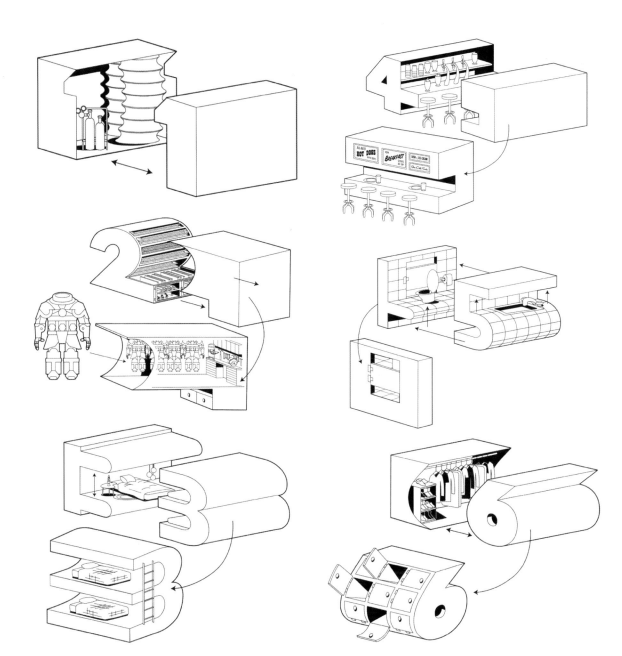

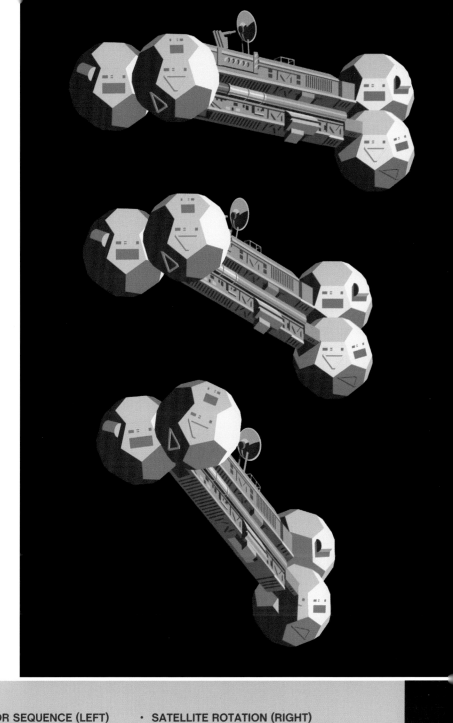

INSPIRATIONAL ART
Marty Baumann

Marty Baumann, another long-time friend of the show, is a brilliantly inventive artist. (He often does work for Pixar, and he is also a blues guitarist.) Marty gives his ideas a very detailed, precise treatment, helping to suggest a reality that doesn't exist yet.

His work can also make everything feel like a toy set from the sixties, which is why he was the first illustrator I asked to help me "break the style" for the new doorway sequence.

- **SATELLITE DOOR SEQUENCE (LEFT)**
  Marty took my initial sketches (see P.56) and expanded them with a ton of fun details and new ideas. We both loved the idea of treating the rooms on the SOL like a big *MST3K* play set. You can see how his designs sort of suggest that vibe, with lots of charming flourishes about how life might work for Jonah and the Bots.

- **SATELLITE ROTATION (RIGHT)**
  Another idea I wanted to explore was having the theater – which is in the two large spheres at one end of the SOL – able to rotate 90% to help change the aspect ratio from the show's original 4:3 to a more modern 16:9. In the end, we decided it was a fun idea, but didn't add enough "payoff" in exchange for the cost.

INSPIRATIONAL ART
Steven Sugar

Steven Sugar is a designer for the wonderful animated series, *Steven Universe*, and has a genuine knack for creating a sense of warmth for the exteriors and interiors of buildings.

So, I really wanted to get his take on what colors he thought would be good for the new Interior on the Satellite of Love.

After all, it's not a very straightforward challenge: How *do* you make the vast, dark reaches of outer space seem warm and welcoming? As you can see in the design above, the answer has a lot to do with color.

- **SATELLITE OF LOVE, INTERIOR (ABOVE)**
  Steven was the one who had the lovely idea of using moonlight to tint the colors onboard the Satellite of Love, and those moonlight blues and purples were to become the de facto colors we used to paint and light the interior of the SOL. As you can see, Steven's early direction also explored the idea of expanding the Bridge of the SOL to make it more of a living room, with comfortable furniture and higher, vaulted ceilings.

- **MOONBASE 13 (TOP)**
  For this early iteration of The Mads' lair, I asked Steven to experiment with including elements that resembled an "Aztec Temple on Mars," which is how sci-fi luminary Harlan Ellison used to describe his home in the Hollywood Hills.

- **REPTILICUS METALLICUS (BOTTOM)**
  I also really loved Steven's take on Reptilicus Metallicus, which had a lovely whimsical quality. We didn't end up using this exact rendering for the final puppet, but it provided a great inspirational direction.

INSPIRATIONAL ART
Crist Ballast

Crist Ballas was a long-time make-up artist at Best Brains during the original run of the show. He has since gone on to be a part of the Academy-award winning make-up team for J.J. Abrams' *Star Trek*.

Early in the concepting process, Crist offered a page-one redesign of Professor Bobo (*above*), showing us a thought-provoking alternative vision of the future.

INSPIRATIONAL ART
Brett Bean

Brett "2D" Bean has a wonderful, unique style, and his work is great at suggesting the relationship between characters.

When he agreed to help with some inspirational art, I was especially looking forward to seeing his interpretation of the dynamic between Kinga, her grand-mother, Pearl, and Pearl's clone, Synthia.

- **INITIAL SKETCHES (LEFT)**
Bean's pencil sketches suggest a few possible directions for the relationship between Kinga and Pearl, with almost Disney-style playfulness alongside some otherwise gothic elements.

- **COLOR TREATMENT (RIGHT)**
Bean expanded one of his directions with a delightful *Beetlejuice* cartoon-style color palette, which has echoes in the final design of the Moon 13 sets.

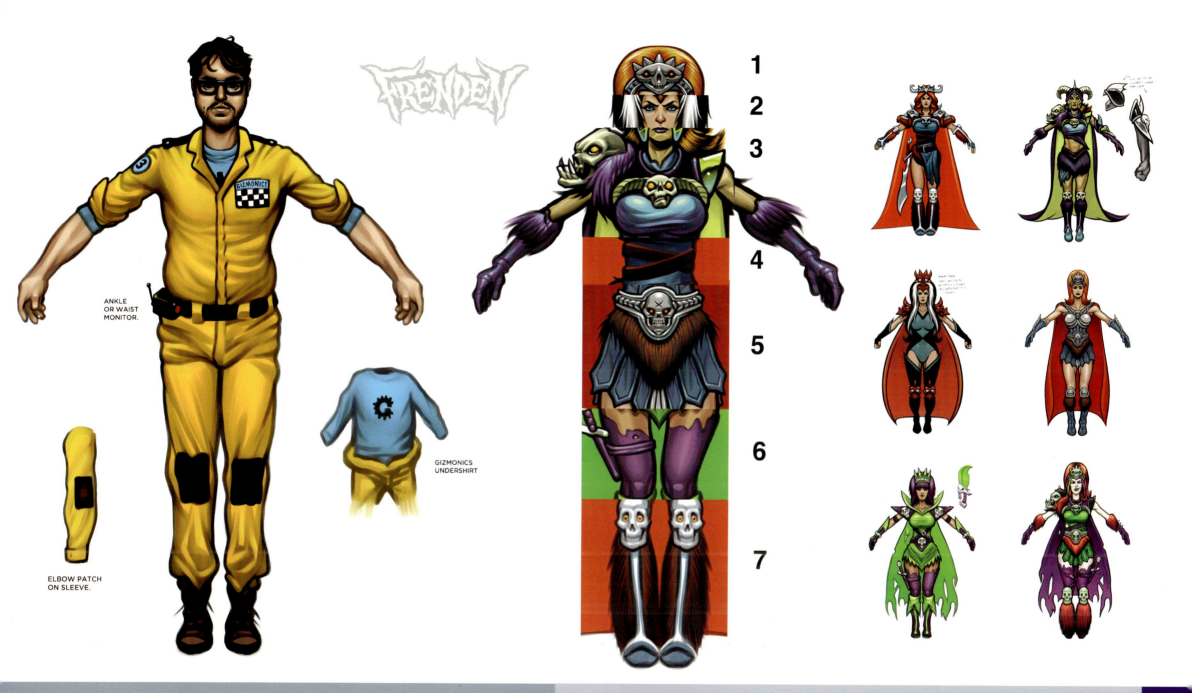

FRENDEN

1
2
3
4
5
6
7

ANKLE
OR WAIST
MONITOR.

GIZMONICS
UNDERSHIRT

ELBOW PATCH
ON SLEEVE.

Ray Frenden

Ray Frenden brought a flashy, punk rock aesthetic to some early versions of Kinga's look as well as Jonah's humble jumpsuit. One thing I appreciate about Frenden's style is the way he's able to simmer down the concept into a very finished "graphic" style.

I also like Frenden's drawings because they're so dimensional and articulate. As you can see, his characters have a lot of shading, and even muscle tone in the neck and arms.

- **JONAH'S GIZMONIC JUMPSUIT (LEFT)**
We considered a lot of colors for Jonah's jumpsuit, but I think Frenden got closest on his first try – a nice, rich goldenrod hue. You can also see that, at the time, we were toying with the idea of a sky-blue Gizmonic shirt underneath.

- **KINGA'S ARMOR OPTIONS (RIGHT)**
Early in the development process, we were exploring the idea of Kinga wearing battle armor, like a character from *Masters of the Universe*, or Lady Gaga.

(Spoiler Alert: I still really like this idea and I am hopeful that we can revisit it in future episodes of the series, live show or comics.)

CONCEPT ART

Seth Robinson

Once you've got a lot of great inspirational art, of course, the next step is to start turning those ideas into **concept art.** If inspirational art is meant to help establish a *mood*, concept art is more like drafting blueprints of how the ideas will actually be realized *on screen.* It needs to be complete enough to hand to costume designers, set builders, prop makers, and other collaborators, so that they know what you're asking them to create.

As we moved into the development of concept art, no one was more critical to the process than Seth Robinson, who has been a key part of the "Alternaversal Vision Team" at the center of bringing back *MST3K.* (You can read more about Seth *and* the Vision Team on P.100.)

One of the most amazing things about Seth is that he understands *all* of the parts of the process, and is comfortable creating both inspirational *and* concept art in a wide range of styles and mediums.

Throughout the process, Seth worked closely with most of our vendors, designers and partners to make sure everyone was on the same page and communicating.

And, as you can see on these pages, Seth is *also* a talented illustrator who contributed many of his own designs, ideas and modifications to the *MST* canon along the way.

- **KINGA & HER CREW (P.26)**
Seth designed Kinga's new costume as part of a larger concept rendering that included Max and the Boneheads. Max's chauffeur costume, seen here, is based on the one worn by Erich von Stroheim in Billy Wilder's *Sunset Boulevard.*

- **FLYING GYPSY (TOP LEFT)**
As we started imagining the sketch segments, Seth put together a concept rendering of Gypsy flying over Copenhagen during a break from *Reptilicus.* We loved the general feeling and style, which I think translated very nicely on screen.

- **SOL SCALE STUDY (TOP RIGHT)**
Using a hybrid of photo elements and concept artwork, Seth whipped together a "scale study" so we could start planning just how a 6'5 Jonah was going to fit on our set alongside his robot friends.

- **PROPS & BOT COSTUMES (BOTTOM ROW)**
Seth often employs a charming pencil style to move rough ideas towards more refined stages, resulting in specs and designs suitable for prop fabricators, costume designers, and set builders.

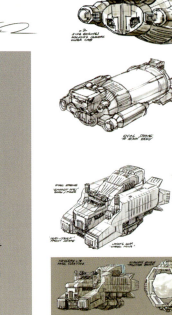

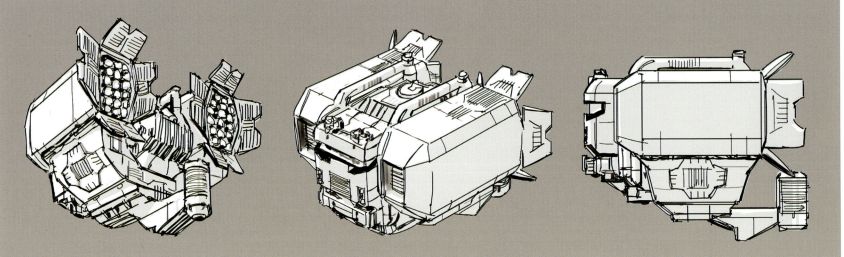

CONCEPT ART
Guy Davis

I first met Guy Davis via Twitter. I'd always been a fan of his comics, such as *The Marquis*, but a few years before the Kickstarter, I found out that Guy was also doing some amazing set design and concept work for folks like Guillermo del Toro.

So, I asked him to do a design for Jonah's Gizmonic space tug, the "Backjack," and each day for the rest of that week, Guy sent me a new concept for Jonah's vehicle via e-mail.

When he got to the final version that Friday, he'd hit on the idea of having rocket gear retrofitted around a semi-truck! It was probably the most Gizmonic thing I'd ever seen!

I knew, right then and there, that I had to hire Guy to design the rest of the new key elements, including our locations, environments, sets, props, furniture, and visiting spaceships.

As you can see, he killed it.

- **BACKJACK VARIATIONS (ABOVE)**
Some of the many concept designs that Guy sent me for the Backjack. While each of them had interesting aspects, we settled on the one that looked most like a semi-truck in space (*top left*). To see how this evolved into the on-screen model, check out P.53!

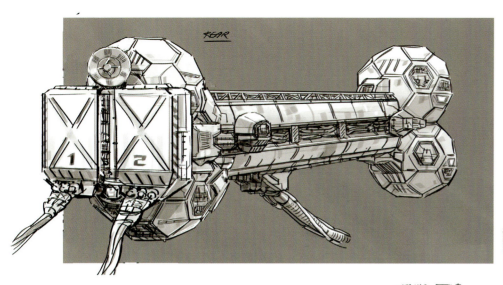

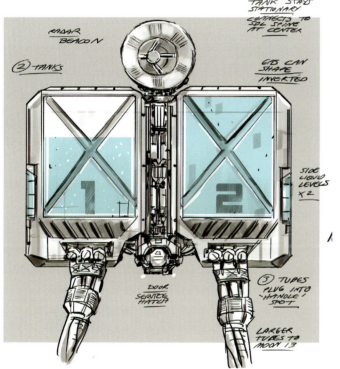

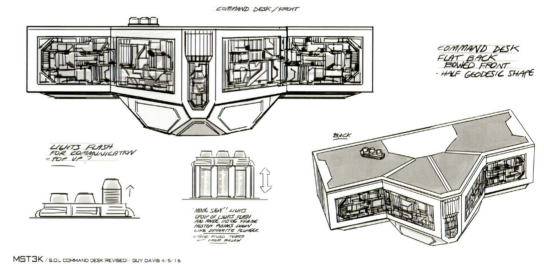

MST3K / S.O.L COMMAND DESK (REVISED) / GUY DAVIS 4/5/16

GUY DAVIS

The Satellite of Love

- **TANKS ON SOL EXTERIOR (TOP LEFT)**
  The reservoirs of Kingachrome attached to the hull of the Satellite of Love.

- **KINGACHROME TANKS (BOTTOM LEFT)**
  Reservoir 1 contains the Kingachrome of the movies that Jonah and the Bots are riffing on. Reservoir 2 contains the Kingachrome that Cambot uses to record the show. Everything on Moon 13 and the SOL runs on liquid Kingachrome... because Kinga decrees it.

- **THE EXPANDED BRIDGE (TOP RIGHT)**
  This concept art shows an expanded vision for the SOL's interior, showing a sunken living room, as well as a rare glimpse of what the ceiling might look like... revealing several hundred yards of Gypsy's tubing and the track Cambot runs along.

- **DESK DETAILS (BOTTOM RIGHT)**
  Guy takes Kingachrome to its logical extreme. You gotta love the piston-controlled iteration of the new movie sign, Moon 13 sign, and commercial sign. Or at least, I do, anyway.

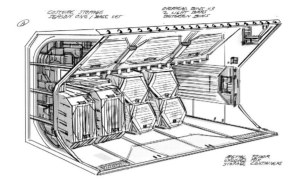
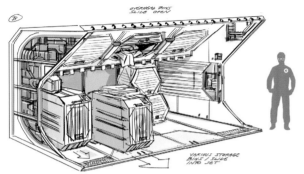
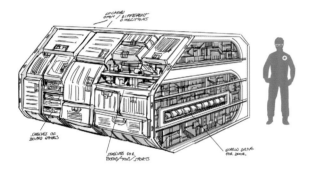
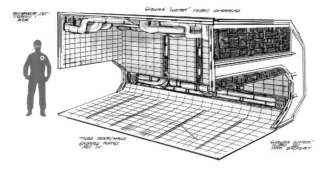
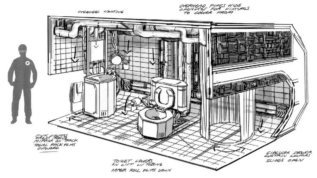
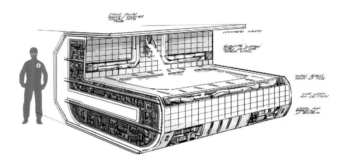
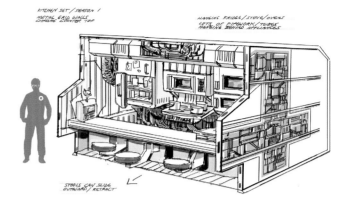
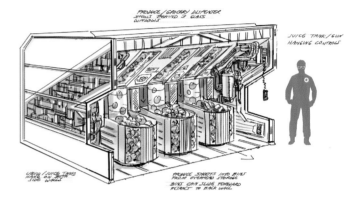

 6  **5** **4**

GUY DAVIS
The SOL Doorway Sequence

As you can tell from my early sketches and Marty's inspirational art (P.21), one of our most ambitious and fun goals for *The Return* was to really build out the Doorway Sequence. Back in the day, it didn't seem to serve a lot of purpose. This time, it seemed like a nice way to suggest some of the details of life on the Satellite of Love, and create spaces we could reference later. These drawings became invaluable to our model makers as they built the actual models that appeared on screen (see P.56).

• DOOR 6: WARDROBE & STORAGE
Since Jonah and the Bots often have elaborate costumes and props in the host segments and sketches, I thought it would be fun to suggest where all of that stuff comes from. This room is kind of like the ultimate "walk-in closet," full of hanging racks and sliding storage bins.

Beneath each room, you can also see Guy's reference illustrations for each door's unique sliding elements, which mirror the number of each room. See? Stylish *and* functional!

• DOOR 5: THE BATHROOM
Part of what makes Guy such a wonderful asset is his focus on the little details. Here in the bathroom, the sink and toilet raise and lower as needed... but he even took care to suggest how the toilet paper roll could be designed to flip out of the way when it's not being used. Those kinds of details gave our model makers a lot of fun direction to work with, and also make these drawings a joy to look at.

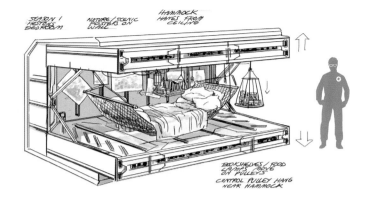

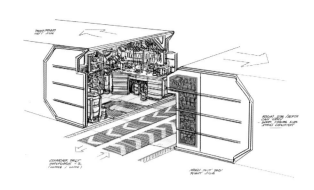

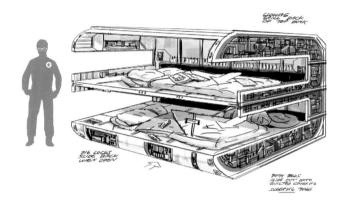

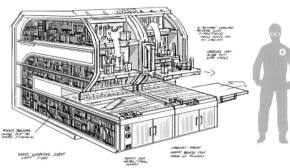

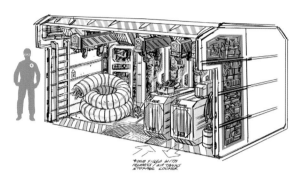

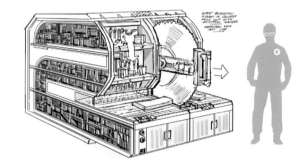

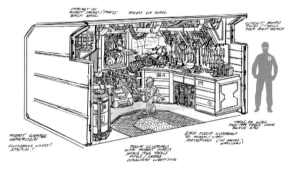

3 **2** **1**

- **DOOR 4: KITCHEN & LARDER**

  If you're *still* wondering how they eat and breathe, and other science facts, this might ease your mind: the updated SOL is equipped with a really wonderful Chef's Kitchen, a diner-style counter with swing-out stools, and even a series of tubes and dispensers that provide Jonah with fresh fruit and groceries that drop into view as Cambot glides by.

- **DOOR 3: SLEEPING QUARTERS**

  The shared bedroom is full of beautiful little ideas and details. After experiment-ing with a rotating circular velvet bed, we settled on the more handmade, Robinson Crusoe-style hammock, with hanging bookshelves and lamps. On the other side, Crow and Servo share bunk-beds. At one point, Crow's bunk even had a spinning comic book rack!

- **DOOR 2: JONAH'S FAB LAB**

  I think Jonah's maker space, or fab-lab, is one of the most important rooms on the whole SOL. As you can see, he's equipped with everything he needs to make props, inventions, and anything else he can imagine. One of my favorite details is the crosscut buzzsaw that tucks away into the upper curve of the room's "2."

- **DOOR 1: BACK 40 & ROBOT WORKSHOP**

  This room represents something kind of like a garage on the SOL. And, just like most garages, it's full of all kinds of junk and bric-a-brac: extra robot parts, tools and circuit boards. On the other side of the room are the SOL's "winter clothes" – helmets, protective suits and air tanks for surface repairs and escape attempts.

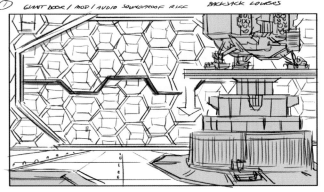

① GIANT DOOR / MOD / AUDIO SOUNDPROOF RIGG   BACKJACK LOWERS

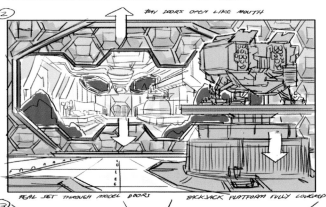

② BAY DOORS OPEN LIKE MOUTH

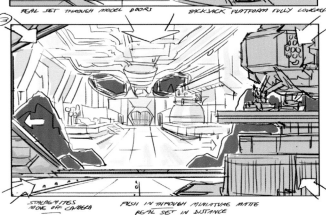

③ REAL SET THROUGH MODEL DOORS   BACKJACK PLATFORM FULLY LOWERED

STALAGMITES MOVE OFF CAMERA   PUSH IN THROUGH MINIATURE MATTE
REAL SET IN DISTANCE

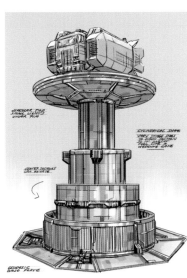

GUY DAVIS
Moonbase 13 & The Show Trap

· BACKJACK ELEVATOR (LEFT)
Guy Davis designed the elevator that lowers the Backjack down to the floor of Moon 13. Then an airlock opens revealing the massive subterranean laboratory and TV studio. Note: This original shot was designed to combine two hanging models "in camera" – the elevator and the Moon 13 ceiling – but we ended up opting for the less expensive method of photographing the elements separately and combining them in post-production.

· MOONBASE 13 (TOP RIGHT)
The sprawling underbelly that is Moon 13. This was the design for a composite shot that featured a hanging model of the ceiling, along with the live action on the sound stage. If you look closely, there's also an easter egg in this drawing: an image of Mark Hamill appears on the God Monitor, since we hoped we'd be able to get him on the show.

· MOON 13 TRAP FACADE (BOTTOM RIGHT)
The idea of the Moon 13 trap façade is to lure in unsuspecting space travelers, then abduct them – ship and all – down into Kinga's underground lair. The temporary-looking construction is based on a style of stunt show façade designed to catch on fire. Simply put: Kinga isn't above using a little movie magic to kidnap someone.

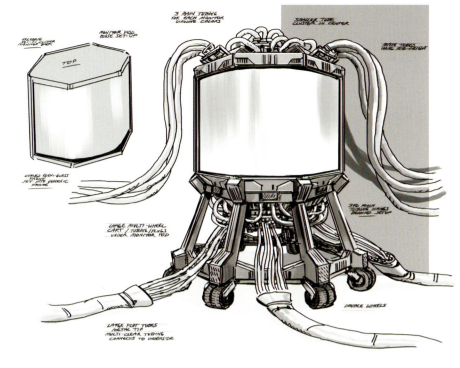
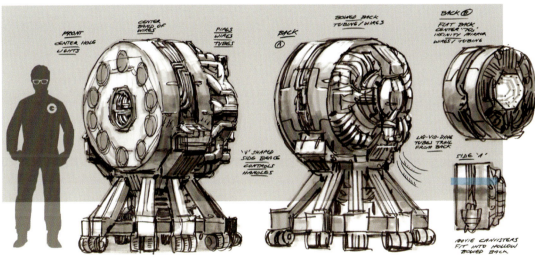
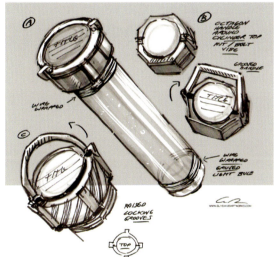

GUY DAVIS
Moon 14 & Kingachrome

• MOON 14 MOVIE SILO (TOP LEFT)
When I look at this drawing, I have to relate again how wonderful it was to have Guy Davis on our team. He has such an amazing sense of reality and manufacturing that these far-out ideas really start to feel "real." As a showrunner and creator, every time I open a new concept illustration from Guy, it's like Christmas – or Hanukkah, or Kwanzaa, or Festivus – all over again.

• GOD MONITOR (TOP RIGHT)
"God Monitor" is an industry term that comes from TV production and means the monitor that the entire production used as a final reference. The God Monitor on Moon 13 is like a big aquarium that holds hundreds of gallons of Kingachrome. I loved this design from Guy, as I think it had a real Jack Kirby vibe; it feels like something M.O.D.O.K. might use to watch CNN while sitting in his doomsday chair.

• KINGACHROME OPERATOR (BOTTOM RIGHT)
For a while we were thinking that maybe the Observers were hanging out and helping Kinga. We later replaced them with Boneheads. However, we *did* build this prop and you can see it briefly in the show open when we first reveal Kinga's lair. A Bonehead holding this camera rig walks in front of the camera to demonstrate that the Mads were, indeed, recording the next shot.

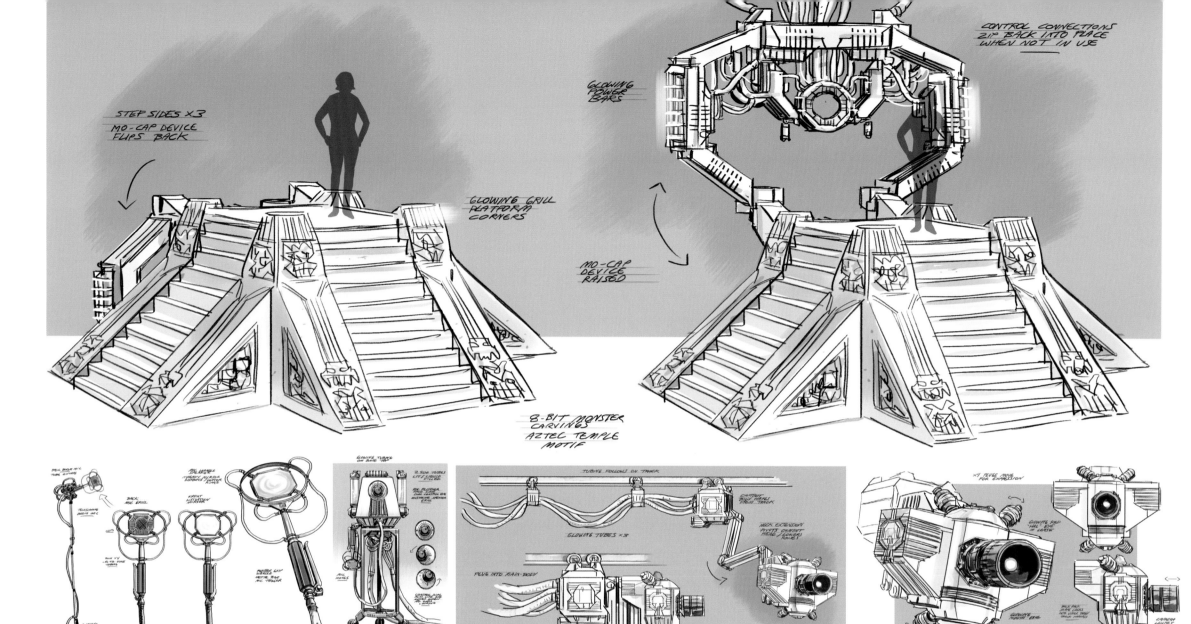

GUY DAVIS

Kinga's Mic, Ziggurat & Cameras

- **KINGA'S ZIGGURAT (TOP)**

This set piece was initially designed to be used for an in-camera effect that would make it look like Reptilicus Metallicus had eaten Jonah during the wedding-scene conclusion of Season 11. (Don't believe me? Take another look at the first sketch of Reptilicus on P.15!)

- **KINGA'S MIC (BOTTOM LEFT)**

All the sound recording equipment and cameras are rigged with an elaborate series of tubes pumping Kinga's Kingachrome liquid. This was meant to be reminiscent of the early days of broadcasting, when everything had a cord attached to it.

- **CAMBOT (BOTTOM CENTER + RIGHT)**

We decided early on that Cambot should be on an overhead track that runs the length of the doorway sequence. The other iterations of Cambot that I worked on were attached to the floor. There *was* that one that floated, but I always wondered why it didn't follow Mike and the Bots wherever they were going and instead just went down the hallway. (I know, I know: I.J.A.S.I.S.R.J.R.)

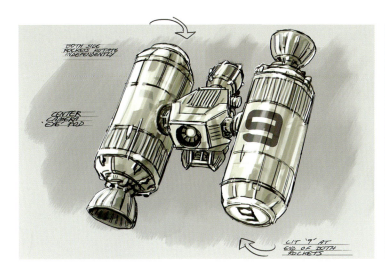

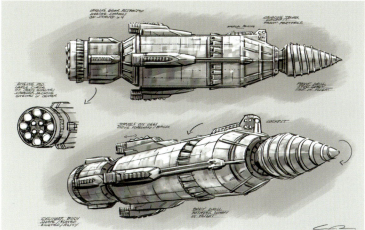

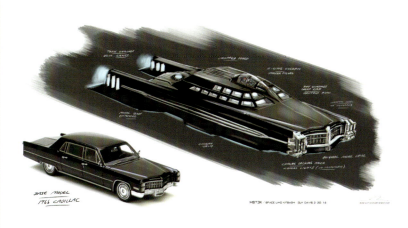

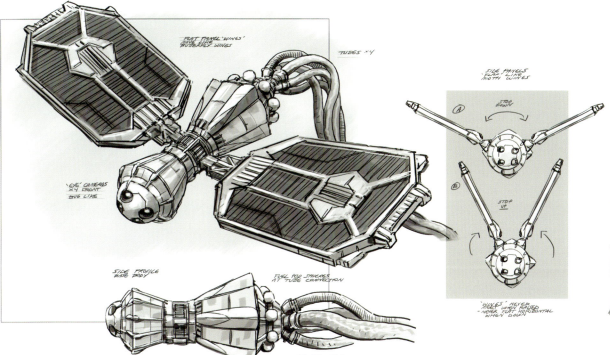

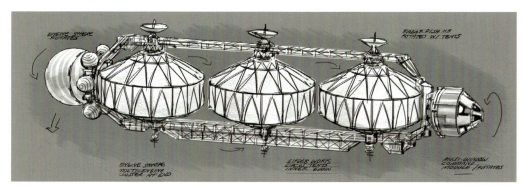

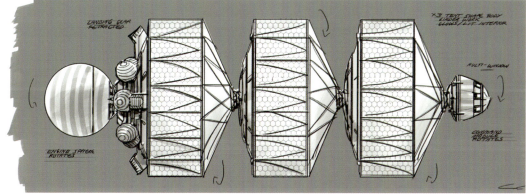

GUY DAVIS

Satellites, Space Probes & Guest Ships

- **ROCKET NUMBER 9 (TOP LEFT)**
  After 30 years we were finally able to visualize the long unseen space probe. Note: The name "Rocket Number 9" is from the song by Sun Ra and his Space Myth Arkestra.

- **IRON BUTTERFLY (BOTTOM LEFT)**
  Some unique details of the Iron Butterfly, Kinga's liquid-media-tethered-drone, with liquid pixel display wings.

- **IRON MOLE (TOP CENTER)**
  The Iron Mole spaceship was one of the easiest ships to concept, in that I just told Guy, "Hey, let's make a spaceship version of the Iron Mole from *At the Earth's Core!*"

- **MASTERSTROKE'S LIMO (TOP RIGHT)**
  I was so fortunate to get Jerry Seinfeld to play space mogul Freak Masterstroke. As you probably know, Jerry is a real car nut, so we spent a little more time than usual to get his space limo design just right.

- **P.T. MINDSLAP'S SHIP (BOTTOM RIGHT)**
  When Mark Hamill agreed to do a cameo, we knew we had to find a really fun part for him. What better role than P.T. Mindslap, ringmaster of the great Space Circus? Here, Guy experiments with the very best design for a spaceship that travels with its own three ring circus.

GUY DAVIS

Gizmonic Institute

- **GIZMONIC EXTERIOR (ABOVE)**

For the opening sequence, I really wanted to reprise the moment in the Comedy Channel era show when the church breaks in two and a large satellite dish comes out. Only now, instead of searching the skies for the SOL, the satellite dish is searching the skies for Jonah and his payload.

So, I asked Guy to give the buildings an early '80s vibe, and this was the amazing design he came back with. Also, the hovercraft was Guy's idea. If you watch closely in the opening sequence, when the hovercraft flies by, it drops its engine.

In this shot you can also see that Guy has included a lot of little details to indicate that the Gizmonic Institute has fallen on hard times, like "FOR RENT" and foreclosure signs... even a pedestrian on the moving walkway wearing a sandwich board.

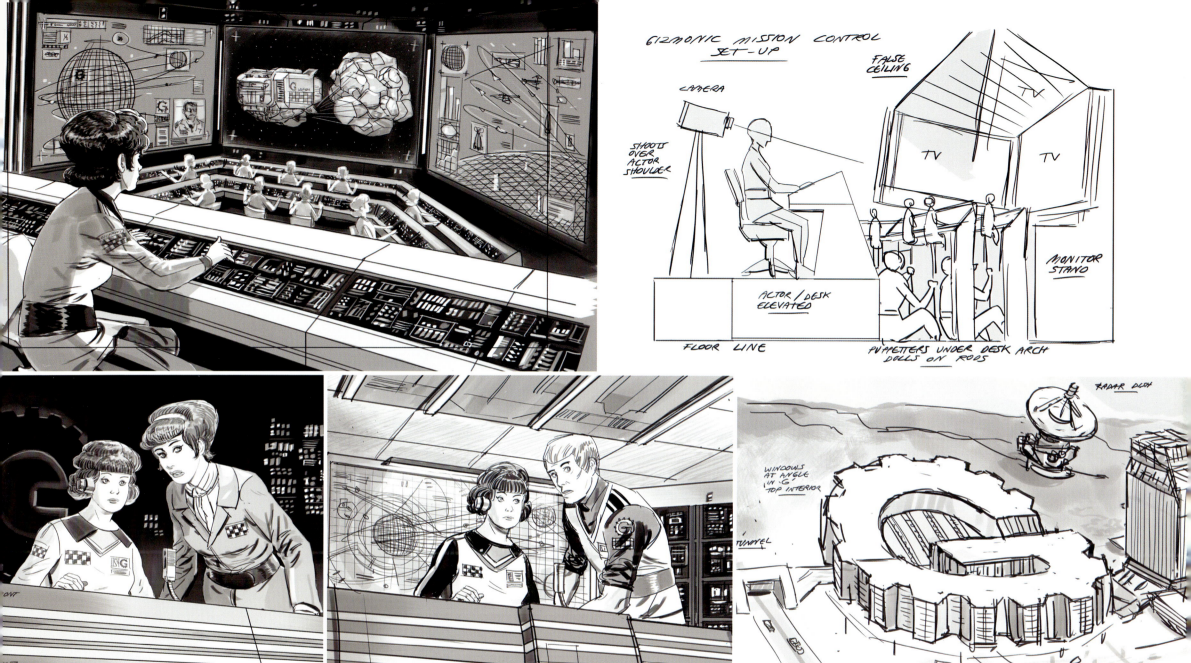

GIZMONIC MISSION CONTROL
SET-UP

FALSE CEILING

CAMERA

SHOOTS OVER ACTOR SHOULDER

TV

TV

TV

ACTOR/DESK ELEVATED

MONITOR STAND

FLOOR LINE

PUPPETEERS UNDER DESK ARCH
DOLLS ON RODS

RADAR DISH

WINDOWS AT ANGLE IN 'G' TOP INTERIOR

TUNNEL

- **GIZMONIC MISSION CONTROL (TOP LEFT)**
We needed a command center at the Gizmonic Institute to show Jonah being tracked on his deep space mining mission by his supervisors at the institute on Earth. The left and center images on the bottom row also show some ideas for the reverse shot, which would eventually feature the fantastic Wil Wheaton and Erin Gray.

- **SHOOTING DIAGRAM (TOP RIGHT)**
Another wonderful thing about Guy is that he doesn't *just* do great concept art, but also does the technical drawings that illustrate how the shot can be captured in the studio. Here, Guy has provided a diagram showing how the camera can capture both a live actor and a model of the set filled with puppets, acting as the Mission Control team below.

- **EARLY CONCEPT (BOTTOM RIGHT)**
Guy's early pass on the main building for Gizmonic Institute. We were talking about the idea of having the Gizmonic Institute feature a large atrium that was built on the inside of a mountain. To accommodate this, Guy amazed and bewildered us all by actually *bending* the Gizmonic building to fold so it was contoured to the side of the mountain.

Sc 001 Panel 5

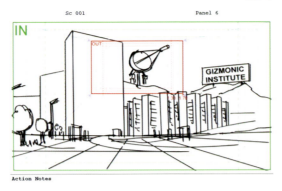

Action Notes

Sc 001 Panel 6

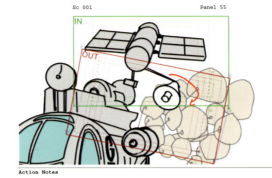

Action Notes

Sc 001 Panel 55

Action Notes

Sc 001 Panel 56

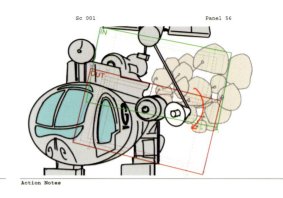

Action Notes

Sc 001 Panel 7

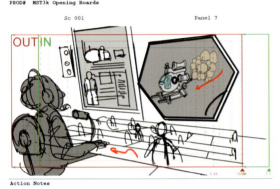

Action Notes

Sc 001 Panel 8

Action Notes

Sc 001 Panel 57

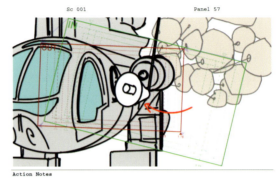

Action Notes

Sc 001 Panel 58

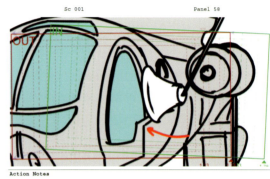

Action Notes

Sc 001 Panel 9

Action Notes

Sc 001 Panel 10

Action Notes

Sc 001 Panel 59

"In the not too distant future"

Action Notes

Sc 001 Panel 60

"In the not too distant future"

Action Notes

JOSH PRUETT
Production Storyboards

Now, once most of the concept art has come together, there's still another important step left before we start building: to put together more detailed **Production Storyboards** that start to help everyone understand *exactly* what we want to put on the screen.

We were fortunate to get the incredible **Josh Pruett** to throw in on the storyboards when he did, as he happened to be between cartoon and publishing gigs, which is rare for him. Josh is so full of good ideas and good vibes, his enthusiasm is simply contagious. And, not only does he know how things translate to the screen, Josh's deft illustrations suggest motion within the still panels of boards. Very important.

When we first sat down to talk about the storyboards, I had just a rough version of the new script for the show open, which we read through together while eating huevos rancheros and drawing new ideas on our napkins. (I wish I still had those to show you.)

Anyway, you can see how some of the sketches in these storyboards borrow directly from the concept work that Guy and Seth provided, and start accounting for important decisions like camera angles.

Sc 001 — Panel 97

Sc 001 — Panel 98
"We got one!"

Sc 001_2 — Panel 27

Sc 001_2 — Panel 28

Sc 001 — Panel 99
"Set the trap!"

Sc 001 — Panel 100

Sc 001_2 — Panel 29
"I should really just relax — for"

Sc 001_6 — Panel 1
"I should really just relax — for"

Sc 001 — Panel 101

Sc 001 — Panel 102

Sc 001_6 — Panel 2
"I should really just relax — for"

Sc 002 — Panel 1
INT. SOL
Joins the bots as Crow looks outside

- **PHASE 1 (P.38, COLUMNS 1 & 2)** These first panels show how we could go about merging the model of Gizmonics and the puppet "Mission Control" with the live action actors for the opening scene.

- **PHASE 2 (P.38, COLUMNS 3 & 4)** Here, the Backjack gets attacked by the insect-like "Iron Butterfly" (the first liquid-media-tethered-drone), which attaches to the SOL and puts a bullhorn on the side of Jonah's cockpit to send him the show's familiar-sounding theme song.

- **PHASE 3 (ABOVE, COLUMNS 5 & 6)** "We got one!" Kinga realizes she's trapped a new patsy for the *MST3K* experiments and signals for the show to begin!

- **PHASE 4 (ABOVE, COLUMNS 7 & 8)** Jonah trucks through the new doorway sequence, onto the bridge of the SOL, and meets his new robot companions. We ended up changing this to have Kinga drop Jonah right into the theater, where we meet the Bots in silhouette.

CONCEPTING

39

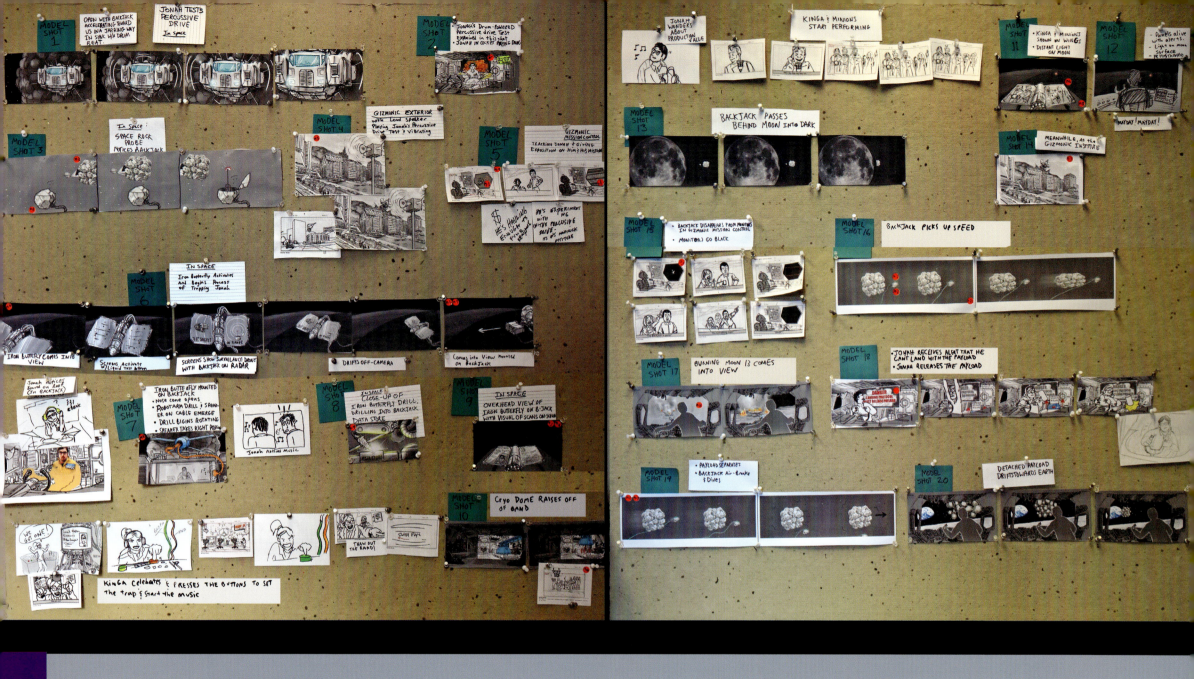

SHOW OPEN

Final Boards

The last real part of the Concepting phase is to assemble the **Final Boards.** (Or, as we called it, "Frankenstein."). During this last stage, we pulled together a lot of different pieces from the concept stage, including Guy Davis' drawings, Josh Pruett's storyboards, my notes, and additional storyboard panels from Seth, and used them to visualize the final version of *Mystery Science Theater's* new opening sequence, or "show open."

This was incredibly helpful, because it lets us integrate all of our finished ideas together into a linear order... or to find out if that was even possible!

(As an aside, I imagine this was probably how animators used to assemble all the early Disney shorts and features.)

Anyway, the idea was that if I could stand next to the Frankenstein boards and walk someone through the show opening with a pointer, and everything meshed together and made sense, we'd know we had successfully joined all these disparate ideas into a unified whole.

Fortunately, it worked!

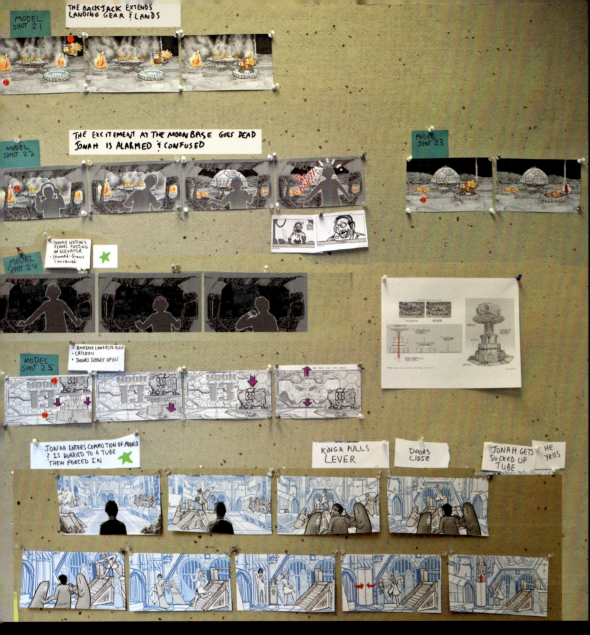

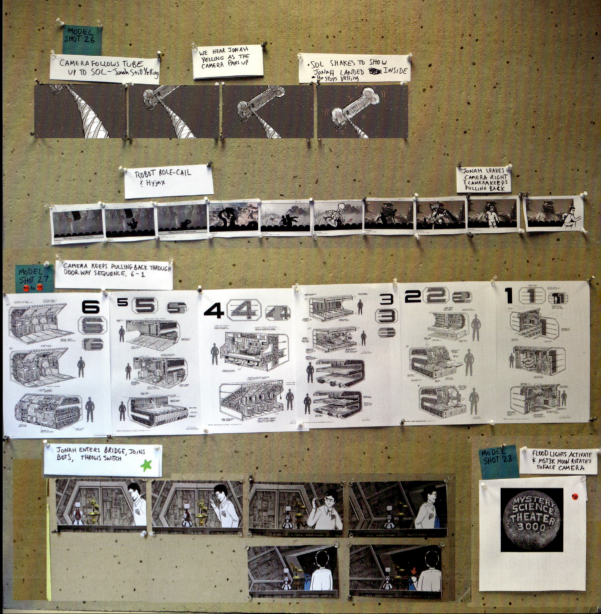

Later in the process, we used these boards, added the original opening theme song, and cut together an "animatic" to make sure everything would fit in the 90 seconds we had allocated for the show open. With a little bit of tinkering, we were able to make it all work… and you can see for yourself how it turned out in the first few minutes of *The Return*!

Of course, even though we moved into the next phase, and started *building* all of these ideas, it doesn't mean we were done with concepting. Most of the time, you keep having new ideas all the way through production… and if you're lucky, you can find ways to include the best ones.

So yeah, that's a look at a lot of the most interesting parts of the first step in the process, the CONCEPTING phase.

The next step, once this is all done, is to use all of these drawings, blueprints and sketches to bring the ideas to life, so that we can put them on the screen. Ready?

Building

The next step is **BUILDING**... and that's one of the biggest parts of *Mystery Science Theater*, because almost everything we do is in-camera. Actually, it's probably easiest to think about *MST* as if it's a live show: for the most part, what you see is what you get.

So, this next section is about bringing all of the ideas from our various sources – like the scripts, drawings, and models – into physical form in the "real world," so that we'll be able to use them on screen in the show.

Naturally, this involves a lot of problem solving, because you have to take all of the ideas from the concepting stage and figure out things like dimensions, materials, proportions, and mechanics, to make sure everything will work the way that it needs to when you're shooting.

I don't know of any other current show that is made this way, with such emphasis on in-cam-era effects. To me, it gives everything a very "live" feel that works really well for comedy.

There's a lot of fun stuff to share from this stage, including a behind-the-scenes look at building **SETS** for the Satellite of Love (P.44), Moon 13 (P.50) and the Backjack (P.52); **ROBOTS** (P.46) and **PROPS** (P.63); and – maybe the most interesting part of the building process – our **MODELS** (P.53), all of which were created by the incredibly talented team at Stoopid Buddy Stoodios, who you might know for their popular animated series, *Robot Chicken*.

BUILDING SETS
The Satellite of Love

As we started thinking about the sets in detail, we knew that we wanted the new SOL to feel reminiscent of the sets from KTMA and the Comedy Central years: basically, a nice background plate that could appear behind our host and robots, but not compete with them visually.

Also, from the very beginning at KMTA, I always wanted to emulate a sort of "Louise Nevelson" style for the set. Nevelson was an influential collage sculptor whose work I first saw at the Walker Art Center in Minneapolis.

Even though the rest of our sets were built right on the soundstage where we shot *The Return*, it was important to build the SOL and its scaffolding within driving distance of the Alternaversal offices in Pennsylvania, where we'd be able to visit and inspect the progress as the set was coming

together. So, to build the SOL and its scaffolding, we worked with Aaron Somers' team, and actually constructed everything first in New Jersey, a few months before we started production on the new episodes. Then, we carefully packed everything up and trucked it across the country.

And yes, I paid the driver a bonus – *Smokey and the Bandit* style – upon safe, on-time, and undamaged delivery of the set and props. Thanks to Sharyl for tracking our driver (P.45, *bottom left*) every mile so we wouldn't worry.

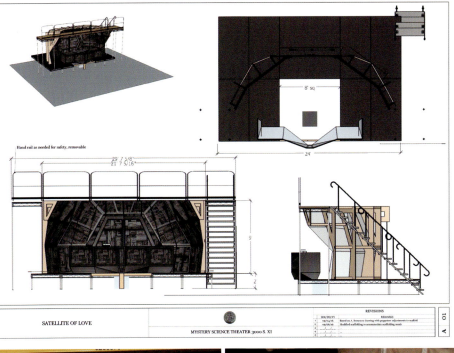

- **SET SCHEMATICS (TOP LEFT)**
  This blueprint gives you a sense of the scale of the entire SOL set, as well as Gypsy's overhead scaffolding.

- **SURFACE ACTION (BOTTOM LEFT)**
  To create the shapes on the surface of the SOL, we designed and cut them from styrofoam with a laser plotter and smoothed the edges with a coat of paint.

- **BUILDING THE FRAME (PHOTO 1)**
  The basic backdrop of the SOL, based on Guy's specifications. The materials used include lauan and plywood attached to an ingenious pine scaffold that can be broken down for shipping and transport.

- **ADDING THE STRUTS (PHOTO 2)**
  With the foundation in place, the team used 1 x 3 pieces of pine to frame the space and add some texture and a stronger "spine."

- **FIRST PAINT (PHOTO 3)**
  Here, the pine molding and lauan plywood hull have been coated with a gunmetal gray primer as a base, with a clean coat of white paint applied on top of it.

- **TEXTURE EXPERIMENTS (PHOTO 4)**
  With a full coat of white paint applied, we begin experimenting with the styrofoam "surface action" shapes, to make sure it creates the right feel for the backdrop.

- **SURFACE TEXTURING (PHOTO 5)**
  Once we liked the general look of the surface shapes, we applied them to the rest of the backdrop, then gave the completed surface another coat of white paint.

- **FINISHING THE DESK (PHOTO 6)**
  With the backdrop finished, we started a similar process for the desk. Bonus: if you look carefully, you might spot a couple of robot faces in the background. (Shhh!)

BUILDING BOTS
Robot Friends

One of the most satisfying parts of *The Return* was getting to revisit the robots, and taking advantage of new ways to make them a little more animated.

In the last 20 years, computer animation and 3-D printing have created all sorts of new opportunities, and let us do a lot more with our old friends. Also, for some reason, it didn't seem as charming for the Bots to have inarticulate arms anymore.

Building on some of the ideas from our initial maquettes (P.16), we also introduced two new faces: M. Waverly and Growler, who quickly became fan favorites.

- **OLD & NEW FRIENDS (TOP, LEFT TO RIGHT)**
Crow looks about the same, but got a few important upgrades, including full-length legs and more capable hands. Servo's arms can move, and he can fly... but only in the theater. Gypsy, despite this image, was redesigned to drop down from above, letting us use her a lot more often, and in more interesting ways. And, of course, the veterans had to learn to share the SOL with new arrivals Waverly and Growler.

- **3-D PRINTED MAQUETTES (BOTTOM LEFT)**
The original maquettes for M. Waverly and Growler were 3-D scanned, so that we could adjust their sizes and proportions on computer. Then, Justin Jacobs 3-D printed their new parts in the appropriate sizes.

- **WAVERLY & GRANT (BOTTOM CENTER)**
M. Waverly's unique voice (and personality) were provided by one of our incredibly talented puppeteers, Grant Baciocco.

BUILDING BOTS

Robot Wardrobe

We knew that *The Return* wouldn't feel like *MST3K* without plenty of elaborate new robot costumes for each episode's host segments, so we were delighted when Beez McKeever, a beloved alum from the original episodes, returned to design and oversee all aspects of the Bots' new wardrobe.

In fact, there were so *many* unique robot costumes that the Bots had their own dedicated costume room. To their disappointment, Crow and Tom Servo *didn't* get their own dressing rooms.

- **ROBOT COSTUMER (TOP LEFT)**
  Beez McKeever at her sewing machine, working a little magic on a garment for Tom Servo.

- **CROW'S COSTUMES (TOP ROW)**
  Some of Crow's more memorable looks from Season 11 included Zombie (*Wizards of the Lost Kingdom*), the title character from *Yongary*, and – with some help from Aaron Somers' team – a full Steampunk redesign (*At The Earth's Core*).

- **ROBOT WARDROBE (BOTTOM LEFT)**
  Here, you can get a sense of just how many robot costumes Beez had to create!

- **SERVO COSTUMES (BOTTOM ROW)**
  Servo also got plenty of new styles in *The Return*, including his "Bot Draper" look (*Avalanche*), his mischievous raccoon (*Cry Wilderness*), and his own steampunk upgrade (*At The Earth's Core*).

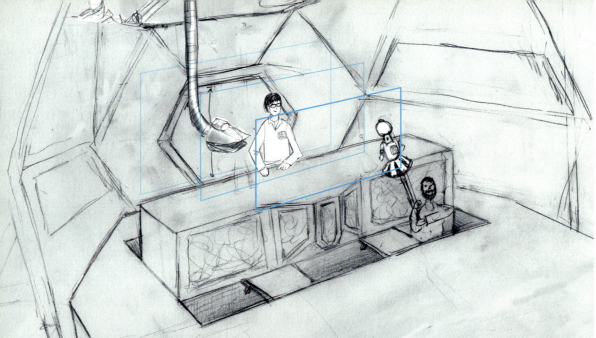

BUILDING SETS

The Bot Trench

Now, this is where we go a little more "behind the scenes." When you're watching *MST*, we want to make sure you're not thinking about the fact that Jonah's robot friends are (technically) elaborate puppets, aided by a hidden team of incredible operators.

For most of the Bots, that required us to build a "Bot Trench" below the desk. And, since we knew these shoots would involve long hours, the first and most important goal was to make the spaces safe and comfortable.

• **TRENCH PLANNING (TOP LEFT)**
Seth Robinson used a draftsman's approach to help us visualize how the bot trench might work, while keeping the operators out of sight. As you can probably guess, the blue boxes help us imaging the camera's frame.

• **BEHIND THE DESK (PHOTOS)**
As you can see in these three photos, the host segments actually require the careful work of an entire team of operators and prop handlers. Some of the most elaborate scenes, like the "Mischievous Raccoons" in *Cry Wilderness* (top right, bottom left) took a lot longer to choreograph and rehearse than shoot!

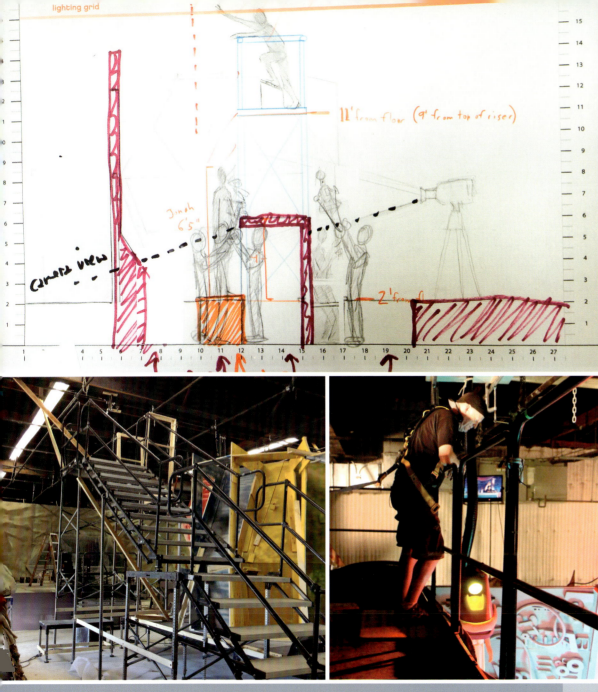

lighting grid

11' from floor (9' from top of riser)

Jonah 6'5"

Camera View

2' from

BUILDING SETS
Gypsy's Scaffold

Even with the Bot Trench in place, we still had another challenge to solve. See, as I think I even said in some of the earliest Kickstarter updates, I really wanted Gypsy to be in the show more this time around. I think the reason we didn't include her as often in the previous iterations was because she was such a big puppet, and really couldn't comfortably fit in the Bot Trench with the other puppets and their operators for any length of time.

We solved that by creating a scaffolding above the bridge of the SOL so she could come and go more easily. Hence, Gypsy shows up much more often in *The Return!*

- **SCAFFOLD PLANNING (TOP LEFT)**
  Once we realized that Gypsy would drop down from overhead, our team began to design a scaffolding that was more along the lines of a Bill Baird marionette rig. As you can see in this planning diagram, one important challenge was figuring out how to also account for Jonah's unique size – 6'5", as of this season! You can also see how Seth and Russ started to anticipate where the cameras would need to be positioned to capture the correct shots.

- **HANGING GYPSY (BOTTOM CENTER)**
  Here, puppeteer Tim Blaney operates Gypsy from the scaffolding above the desk.

- **SCAFFOLD VIEW (RIGHT)**
  This side view gives you a sense of just how massive the final scaffolding was.

49

MOON 13

MYSTERY SCIENCE THEATER 3000 S. XI

BUILDING SETS
Moonbase 13

As you saw in Guy Davis' sketches (P.32), this set was designed to suggest an unspooling gestalt moment when you first see it appear in the show open. Jonah, thinking he was rescuing someone, is instead shanghaied into the center of a TV show theme song, where he has become the unwitting star.

To support the scene, I really wanted a subterranean kingdom vibe, suggesting a secret world going on underground.

To quote Tom Waits' song, "Underground":

They're alive, they're awake /
While the rest of the world is asleep /
Below the mine shaft roads, it will all unfold /
There's a world going on underground

I was also trying to evoke a moment similar to those Sid and Marty Kroft shows like *Lidsville,* when the nice, normal kid sees an unexpected fantasy world unfold. So, by design, the Moon

13 set was supposed to be big enough to accommodate the well-funded TV studio vibe of Kinga's world: a talk show set, the Skeleton Crew band and the pageantry of the Ziggurat.

Of course, that meant this set was much too big to manufacture ahead of time. So, Kinga's lair was built right on the LA soundstage where we shot, just 4 days before we started filming. Check out P.77 to see how it all came out.

- **MOON 13 SET RENDER (P.50, TOP LEFT)**
Aaron Somers did an early render in Sketch-Up of the Moon 13 set. These 3-D renderings are important, so that we can be sure all of the ratios and dimensions work before the crew starts building.

- **FACING SETS (P.50, TOP RIGHT)**
If you look carefully, you can also see that this photo was shot from behind the desk of the SOL. Just like we did back at Best Brains, we thought it would be good for the two sets to face each other. So, when we shot segments on the SOL, the cameras were actually right in the middle of Moon 13.

- **TIME LAPSE (LEFT)**
We left a time-lapse camera set up during most of the set construction. Here, you can see a sequence of four shots showing how the set build progressed over the course of a few long days (and nights).

- **PANORAMIC MOON VIEW (RIGHT)**
These two panoramic shots give you a sense of the scope of the Moonbase 13 set during Season 11. (As you'll see later, we set things up a bit differently in Season 12.)

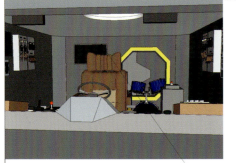

BACK JACK COCKPIT

MYSTERY SCIENCE THEATER 3000 S. XI

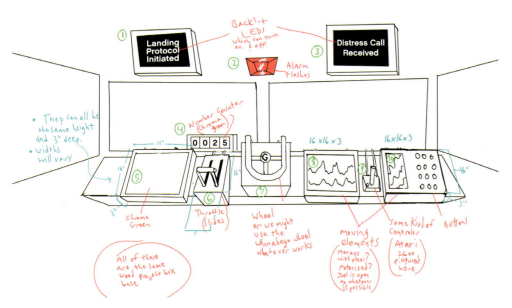

BUILDING SETS
The Backjack Cockpit

Even though most of *The Return* was shot on just two sets – the SOL and Moonbase 13 – there was one additional location that we knew would be important for setting up the new version of the show: the Backjack.

- **PLANNING THE BUILD (TOP LEFT)**
Like Moonbase 13, the interior of the Backjack's cockpit was built entirely on our soundstage in Los Angeles. Here, you can see a concept render that production designer Justin Lieb made in Sketch-Up.

- **CONSOLE (BOTTOM LEFT)**
To help guide the set building team, Seth assembled this diagram showing the various elements we wanted to include on Jonah's dashboard console.

- **BUILDING THE COCKPIT (RIGHT)**
These two photos show you a near-complete version of the Backjack cockpit, prior to lighting.

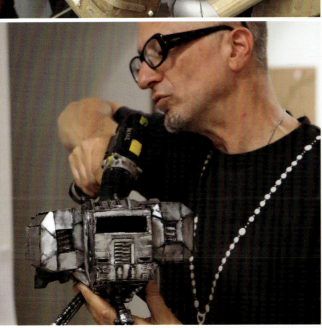

BUILDING MODELS
The Backjack Exterior

So yeah, when you see the Backjack flying through space in the show open, with Jonah at the controls, what you're *actually* seeing is some footage we shot of Jonah with the camera outside of the cockpit set.

This footage is then composited into the model of the Backjack made by our friends at Stoopid Buddy Stoodios. We also had to make a smaller version of the Backjack for the shot where it lands in Kinga's trap, which you can see in the bottom left photo.

- **CARDBOARD & PAINT (TOP)**
  Here, you can get a look at the cardboard foundation of the Backjack (*top left*), as well as a reference photo of the finished model, complete with paint and accessories. See the greenscreen panel inside the windshield? That's where we insert the footage of Jonah in the cockpit. And: *voila*: Jonah appears to be piloting a cardboard model ship 1/50th of his size!

- **MINI-BACKJACK (BOTTOM LEFT)**
  We also needed a smaller replica model of the Backjack for the shot where it lands on the moon as part of Kinga's trap.

- **MORE ANGLES (BOTTOM RIGHT)**
  To really appreciate how talented our modelmakers are, you need to see their work from multiple angles.

BUILDING MODELS
The Moon

OK, so the Moon was probably the most critical redesign of the show for me – but deciding what to do with it was also one of the trickiest decisions!

See, the original version of the *MST3K* moon (*top left*) had served us well, and become a kind of icon for *MST*, so I didn't want to move too far away from it. But, at the same time, it was also starting to look a little worn around the edges – literally!

So, once the Kickstarter succeeded, we knew we had to start figuring out what to do with it.

To start, I asked my friends at House Industries to take a crack at the re-design, and discussed it with their co-founders, Rich Roat – to whom this book is dedicated – and Andy Cruz.

After a few discussions, Rich and Andy handed the task to fabricator and designer Adam Cruz, who started by creating a new computer model of the lunar surface. Once we saw that his digital model did a wonderful job of re-creating both the topography of the moon *and* the typography of the original *MST* moon, we knew we were close... and Stoopid Buddy took it from there!

- **MOON PHASES (TOP ROW, L TO R)**
  1. The original *MST3K* Moon logo
  2. Gary Glover's illustrated adaptation
  3. Andy Cruz's digital model
  4. Stoopid Buddy's first pass
  5. Stoopid Buddy's final version
  6. The finished moon, lit for cameras!

- **CRAFTING THE MOON (BOTTOM)**
  The team at Stoopid Buddy did an exceptional job refining every last detail of the new moon's texture by hand.

BUILDING MODELS

The Satellite of Love

The other major redesign we needed to get right, of course, was The Satellite of Love.

Working from Guy Davis' wonderfully detailed art direction (P.29), the new version was constructed at Stoopid Buddy Stoodios, in Burbank, CA, and we couldn't be more pleased with how it turned out.

- **BUILDING THE SOL (TOP LEFT)**
  Like all of the models, the first step was to construct the foundational structure out of cardboard. Here, Christopher Herndon (wearing a Gizmonic Institute hardhat) is marking some adjustments in pencil.

- **INNER WORKINGS (TOP RIGHT)**
  With the surface panels removed, you can see the concealed wires and parts that light up the model. You can also see the box-shaped "movie-length" reservoir of Kinga-chrome, Kinga's ineffective and messy recording medium, at the far left end of the station.

- **TETHERING (BOTTOM LEFT)**
  Here, Christopher works with Huy Vu to attach the SOL's special coupling unit, which tethers it to Moon 13 via the umbilicus, trapping it on the dark side of the moon.

- **DETAILED FINISH (BOTTOM RIGHT)**
  The near-finished model, complete with paint and detail work.

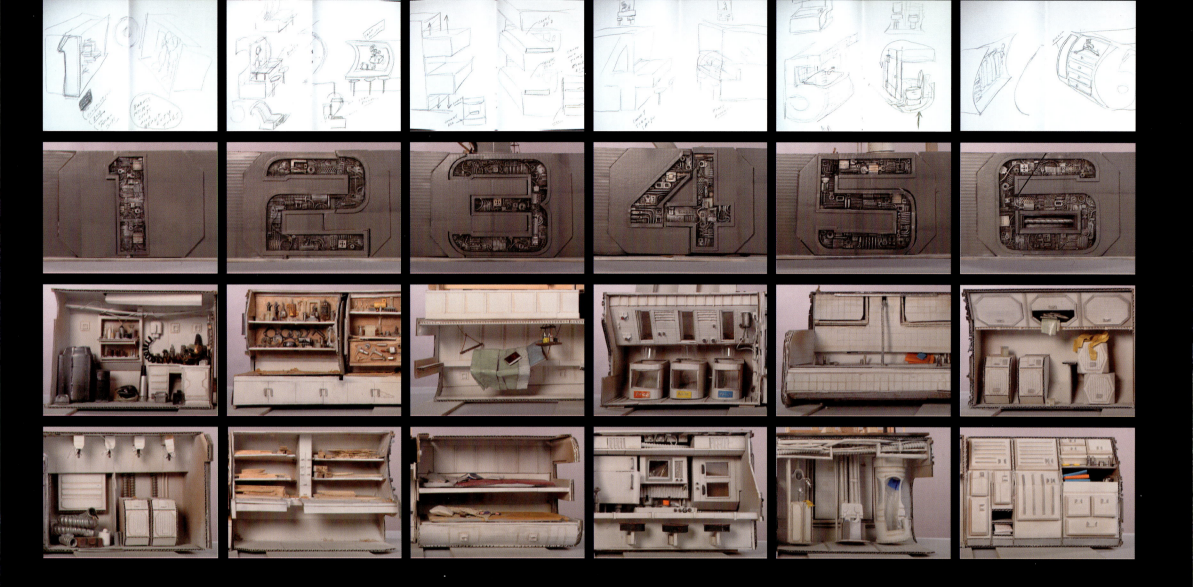

BUILDING MODELS

The Doorway Sequence

While it would be hard to choose a favorite from all of the amazing models that Stoopid Buddy created for us, the podbays in the Doorway Sequence are among the best.

Working from Guy Davis' detailed directions (P.30), the pros at Stoopid Buddy did an astonishing job dialing in the perfect scale for the miniatures, making the podbays and doors big enough to capture the details, but small enough to shoot the finished models on the miniature stage.

- **ORIGINAL SKETCHES (ROW 1)**
  These sketches represent the very earliest versions of my ideas for the doorway sequence. There are some fun details here that we didn't end up keeping. For example, in the first sketches for Podbay 2, Tom and Crow have each set up competing food stands across from each other. You can also see that, even in the first sketches, we settled on the idea of the doors being shaped like numbers.

- **THE DOORS (ROW 2)**
  Even though each door only appears onscreen for a few seconds, Stoopid Buddy took incredible care to get even the littlest elements just right.

- **THE PODBAYS (ROWS 3 & 4)**
  Here, you can see our close-up reference photos of the finished model for each podbay, giving you a sense of how much care and detail went into these models.

- **SETTING THE FOUNDATION (TOP LEFT)**
The original cardboard foundations for each room, before Stoopid Buddy started adding paint, accessories and details. Podbay 6 is open and under construction.

- **FURNISHING THE PODS (TOP RIGHT)**
Looking at all of the small, detailed elements in each podbay felt a lot like playing with an elaborate, one-of-a-kind dollhouse. Here, you can see some of the elements being build for Podbay 6.

- **PODBAY 3: THE BUNKS (RIGHT, ROW 3)**
Can you guess which bunk is Crow's and which one is Servo's? Tom gets the top bunk because he can fly. Also, his sleeping bag is red; Crow's is gold.

- **BUILDING THE PODS (BOTTOM ROW)**
Huy Vu mixes up some custom blended paint that will be used to add texture and detail to the models for each room.

- **LINING THEM UP (BOTTOM RIGHT)**
On the bottom right, Mike Murnane and Huy Vu discuss the configuration of the podbay sequence, since all of the rooms will need to line up just right when we shoot the actual flythrough sequence for the show. (You can see that on P.69!)

BUILDING MODELS
Moonbase 13

Moonbase 13 is a bit of a love-letter to *Space 1999* and the modelwork of Derek Meadings, who may have been the greatest model builder who ever lived.

Of course, our strict adherence to the use of cardboard may inhibit us from winning any awards in this field.

- **CARDBOARD FOUNDATION (TOP LEFT)**
  Here, Stoopid Buddy has constructed the skeleton of Moonbase 13 from cardboard and paper, based on Guy's concept art (see P.32).

- **FINISHED COMPONENTS (BOTTOM LEFT)**
  Note the green screen inside the windows, so that we could add Kinga's unconvincing shadow animations to complete the trap. Remember, this is just for show: the *real* Moon 13 is beneath the surface.

- **PAINTING THE SURFACE (TOP RIGHT)**
  The entire surface of the moon was carefully crafted and painted by hand to give it the perfect moon-like texture.

- **FAKE FIRE (BOTTOM RIGHT)**
  An in-camera fire effect on one of the landing platforms. Later, this element is combined with digital smoke to complete the illusion. And, by the way, it's *all* an illusion.

BUILDING MODELS
Moon 14

Moon 14, of course, is the level beneath Moon 13. (This is obviously for safety reasons, what with the weight of the massive silos that hold the movie-length volumes of Kingachrome and all.)

The designs for Moon 13 and Moon 14 were probably inspired by the original Batcave from the Adam West version of Batman. If you squint at the silo you can almost see the "Atomic Core" from the 1966 Batman series.

- **BUILDING THE RESERVOIR (LEFT)**
  Stoopid Buddy came up with an ingenious method to show the Kingachrome liquid emptying from the silo: building an off-camera reservoir and pump! We were able to adjust the speed of the liquid emptying in post, creating the overall impression that Ardy was pumping the fluid up to the SOL. ("Movie in the hole!")

- **COLORING THE TANK (RIGHT)**
  Originally, we imagined we'd use food coloring to give each movie a different liquid color. Instead, Stoopid Buddy cleverly installed a waterproof hot tub light into the bottom of the silo. Then, they just changed the color of the light by hitting a remote, and then swapped the poster for each film on the outside of the tank! (Pretty smart for a company that calls itself "Stoopid," huh?)

BUILDING MODELS
Gizmonic Institute

At the start of Season 11, the Gizmonic Institute has fallen on hard times and is *just* about to be sold off as low-cost office space.

Jonah's deep space precious metals mining mission was the Institute's last hope to avoid going bankrupt.

- **CARDBOARD ARCHITECTURE (LEFT)**
  Here, you can see a lot of the initial cardboard model work that went into making the Gizmonic campus. Part of what makes Stoopid Buddy so wonderful is their attention to perfecting even the smallest details.

- **CHURCH BROADCAST (TOP RIGHT)**
  Unpainted Scandinavian-style church that breaks in two, and houses a giant radar dish; this is an homage to the show open in the early seasons of the series.

- **CAMPUS LAYOUT (BOTTOM RIGHT)**
  Here, all of the pre-scenic cardboard elements are arranged on a plywood base to give a sense of the entire campus layout.

- **PAINTING THE "G" (TOP LEFT)**
Artist Shayna Rae Newsome, using a dry brush technique to apply details to the cardboard Gizmonic Institute. As you'll see in the next section, there are even lights hidden inside the building structure so that the windows can light up during our final model shoot.

- **FINISHED CAMPUS (TOP RIGHT)**
The near-finished Gizmonic Institute campus. As you can see, there's a road that passes through the mountain, as well as a building facade, suggesting that the mountain is hollow. Which it is.

- **FINISHED SCENERY (BOTTOM)**
Close-ups of model details for buildings, mountains, and trees around Gizmonic Institute. Note the mid-eighties vibe of the architecture, indicating Gizmonics started just prior to the launch of *Mystery Science Theater 3000*, which started in 1988.

BUILDING MODELS
Ships & Satellites

- **IRON BUTTERFLY (LEFT)**
  Detail of Kinga's liquid-media-tethered-drone, The Iron Butterfly, during the fabrication process.

- **NEVILLE'S CAR (TOP LEFT)**
  Neville LaRoy is a wildly-successful space magician. We felt his car should reflect that.

- **OBSERVER'S SHIP (TOP CENTER)**
  The Observer's ship: A brain-shaped flying saucer that would make Ed Wood sit up and take notice!

- **WIDOWMAKER (TOP RIGHT)**
  Special care went into reprising the Widow-maker with lovingly detailed sculpts of Pearl, Brain Guy, and Bobo from earlier seasons.

- **MINDSLAP'S CIRCUS (BOTTOM CENTER)**
  Here you can see Mike Murnane's handiwork, with over a hundred cardboard trusses added for texture and realism. (I know, that's ridiculous. A three-ring circus spaceship that has realism.)

- **IRON MOLE (BOTTOM RIGHT)**
  Detail of Doug McClure's Iron Mole from *At the Earth's Core*. Yeah, it also flies through space if need be.

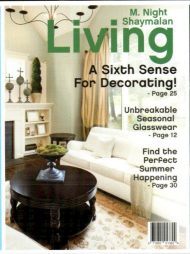

BUILDING PROPS

Props & Inventions

- **PAINTING BRAINS (TOP LEFT/CENTER)**
Propmaster Caroline Louis, hand-painting brains for each of the backers who attended Kinga's wedding as our Observer guests. And yes, they got to keep the brains!

- **PROP DESIGN (BOTTOM, LEFT x4)**
Seth's contributions include the design for Dr. Crow's Edible Silica Packets, *M. Night Shyamalan Living*, and Max's portrait of Kinga. The Cubist portrait of Servo was provided by writer, and Seth's wife, Mary Robinson.

- **WOODCUT MOUNTAIN (MIDDLE RIGHT)**
One of our beautiful laser-cut wooden standees, designed by Seth Robinson.

- **TURKEY THEREMIN (BOTTOM RIGHT)**
This invention was suggested by one of our longtime *MST*ie-turned-writers, Ashley Holtgraver, before we even started writing the season. You might remember that she also performed her "Bring Back MST3K" theme during our Kickstarter Turkey Day Marathon!

- **SPACE SQUID (TOP RIGHT)**
If you look closely, this was made using a spare Tom Servo head that was laying around the Puppetry Garage. The tentacles are made from some plastic kinetic snakes I bought on Amazon.

- **CEREAL BOXES (BOTTOM RIGHT)**
We needed cereal boxes for Crow and Servo's mischievous raccoons to destroy during *Cry Wilderness*. My illustrator friend, Kirk Demarais, designed "Chocolate Crows" (the first box shown above) as an example of what they should look like; Caroline Louis and her team created the rest.

PHASE THREE
Shooting

Once we're done building everything we've envisioned, we're ready for one of the most involved parts of the process: **SHOOTING!**

For a lot of television series, shooting isn't really the end of the line, because so much additional work is done in post-production through editing and special effects. But for *Mystery Science Theater,* it's like I said: we try to do as much "in-camera" as we can, so that what we see when we shoot is what you see on the screen.

Of course, that puts a lot of extra pressure on the entire crew to get everything just right. So, this is when the meter really starts running, because you're working to stay within your budget and on schedule. This is also where the costs really start to add up: between renting studio space, paying the performers, and having a top-flight crew, there's a lot to account for.

That's where our partners at Abominable came in. A few years earlier, I had met Jon Stern and his team at Abominable when I was working on Paul Feig's *Other Space,* and I was just really impressed with their entire crew. So, when I knew we would get to make more *MST* – and

that we were probably going to shoot the new episodes in Los Angeles – I immediately knew I wanted to work with them. Now that we've done two seasons together, I can tell you: we made the right choice.

Anyway, between our team at Alternaversal and our amazing partners at Abominable Studios, Stoopid Buddy and Shout! Factory, everything came together... and in the end, we all had a pretty wonderful experience recording the show.

In this section, you'll get a closer look at how we worked with Stoopid Buddy Stoodios to shoot our **MODELS** (P.66) and our **SILHOUETTES** (P.76), along with a sneak peek at life behind-the-scenes **ON SET** (P.70). I also want to tell you a little more about what it was like to work with **JONAH** (P.72), our amazing **ROBOT TEAM** (P.74), our incredible **MADS** (P.78), and some of our very **SPECIAL GUESTS** (P.80).

So yeah... we've got MOVIE SIGN!

MST3K   MODEL SHOOT

ROLL A 04
(SD)A 03

moon
Element 1

TAKE 1

Director J.HODGSON
Camera H.K.SUN

Date 9/15/16   MOS

SHOOTING MODELS
Stoopid Buddy Stoodios

A few weeks before our main shoot with the cast, we had our miniature model shoot, over at Stoopid Buddy Stoodios. Once all of our creations were set up on their model stage, the team applied their expert skills to breathe life into a world made of cardboard. Making that happen involved a very unusual pair of techniques: very *simple* in-camera animation combined with very *sophisticated* lighting.

As the showrunner, I had double duty, as I was supervising the model shoot while working on an audio mix in the lounge of Stoopid Buddy Stoodios.

Fortunately, Seth Robinson was there to assist me with watching the clock, tracking the shots, and making sure everything from the script to the animatics were being addressed just right.

- **SHOOTING THE MOON (LEFT)**
One of the single most important models we needed to light and shoot was the updated *MST* moon, which doesn't just appear in the opening sequence of the show, but also serves as our show's official logo. So, to make sure we got it right, we handed over the task of lighting and shooting it to the Stoopid Buddy team. As you can see by the exquisite photos, the lighting gives it an austere, icy, and more realistic vibe, while also demonstrating our motto for the design of *The Return*: "New but familiar."

STOOPID BUDDY

Gizmonic Institute

- **GIZMONIC CAMPUS (LEFT)**
Here, you get a good look at the final setup of the Gizmonic Institute campus, complete with pedestrians, cars, and interior lighting in some of the buildings. You'll also see that we're using a motion-control camera. This makes everything *much* easier, because you get an identical camera pass for each shot. Back in the day, we had to do this by hand!

- **MISSION CONTROL (RIGHT)**
At the top, you can see the finished model and lighting for Gizmonic Mission Control. In the middle, you can see that our Mission Control crew was actually populated with off-brand Barbie dolls. (We had to save money at every opportunity.)

- **SHOOTING CONTROL (BOTTOM RIGHT)**
Our model director of photography, Helder K. Sun, surveying the model of Gizmonic Mission Control. This might give you a better sense of just how many people are involved in making even the *quickest* model shots look right on screen.

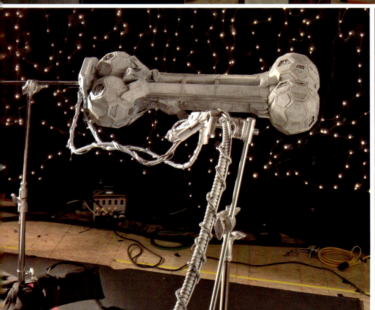

STOOPID BUDDY

Space Ships & Model Sets

- **LIGHTING UP SPACE (TOP LEFT)**
Notice how the almost glaring "sunlight/moonlight" bounced off the Backjack and its payload to emulate the lighting of space.

- **THE SATELLITE (BOTTOM LEFT)**
You can see how the Satellite of Love is held up on a metal C-stand so that the umbilicus cable can tether the SOL to Moonbase 13.

- **MOONBASE 13 (BOTTOM CENTER)**
At the very left, you can see the bottom of the umbilicus tether. Next to it is a neat "in-camera" fire effect we created using a fan, fabric, and LED lights.

- **DIGITAL ANALOG (TOP RIGHT)**
Laser-cut pieces of lauan wood are painted with day-glo colors and hung over a black backdrop to simulate computer graphics for the screens in Mission Control

- **NINJA CREW (MIDDLE RIGHT)**
We thought about putting Christmas lights on the crew's hoodies so they would blend in with the starfield. Then we realized we may have been overthinking it.

- **MOVIE TANKS (BOTTOM RIGHT)**
We used the original poster art as labels for each of the Kingachrome silos, swapping in the correct poster for each shot.

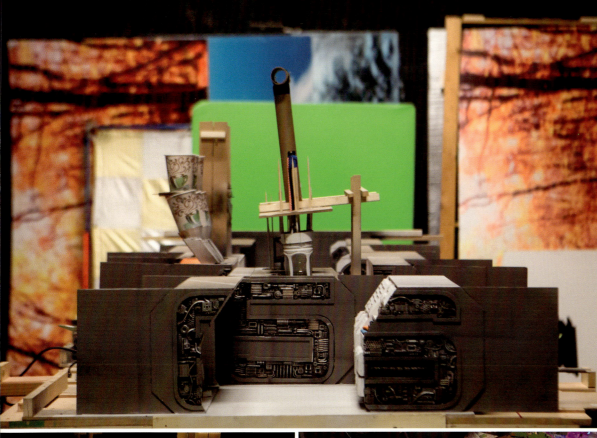

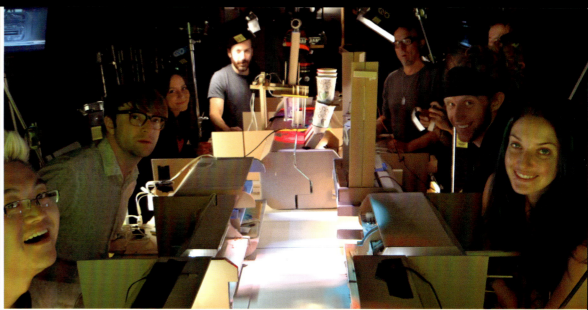

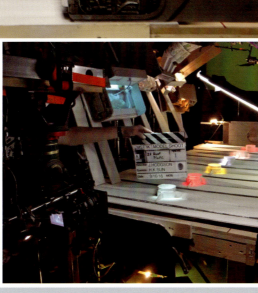

STOOPID BUDDY

The SOL Doorway Sequence

While some of these images might take a little bit of time to decipher, they give you a true "behind the scenes" view of one of our most complicated model sequences, and show how much time and visual artistry are put into lighting a model and bringing it to life.

- **THE CORRIDOR (LEFT)**
The two photos on the left give you a sense of just how long the combined doorway sequence models are – just under 20 feet! For reference, that's about half as long (and *twice* as complex!) as our earlier doorway models.

- **THE CREW (TOP RIGHT)**
All hands on doors! (Except for me. I took the picture.) If you watch the doorway sequence in the context of the TV show, you'll see each podbay has at least two unique "in-camera" animated elements as you pass through.

- **LIGHTING IT UP (BOTTOM RIGHT)**
Here, you can get a good look at the colors of lighting our model director, Helder K. Sun, used to make each podbay look just right.

SHOOTING ON SET
The Satellite of Love

In late September 2016, after months of preparation and planning, the "main event" finally began: shooting sketches with Jonah and the Bots on the new Satellite of Love set, in a small studio that Abominable rented out for the job in Hollywood, CA.

We had two main stages. The smaller one was set up with bluescreen, which we used to shoot our "special guests" who appeared in their unique ships, and greenscreen, which we used to record the silhouette footage for the theater segments. The *larger* soundstage was the home of the new Satellite of Love... which, as it turned out, was positioned directly opposite the set for Moonbase 13. (So yeah, whenever we were shooting in one location, our crew was actually standing in the other.)

Anyway, once we were on set, it really became clear to everyone we were shooting a highly "evolved" version of *Mystery Science Theater*.

Which still isn't saying much.

As you can see here, even simple-looking shots, like the Satellite of Love, got the love and attention of a full crew. And beautiful lighting, to boot!

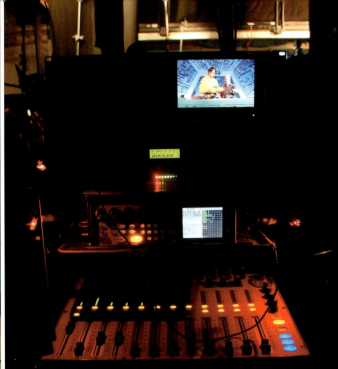

12.05.18.03

ROLL A27 SCENE 101-5/A5 TAKE 1
PROD MST3K
DIR JOEL HODGSON & ROB COHEN FPS
CAM FRANK BARRERA DATE

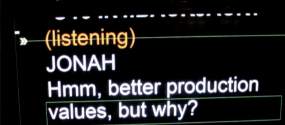

(listening)

JONAH
Hmm, better production values, but why?

- **ONE-TAKE WONDERS (P.70)**
  Recording each sketch in one take, with a single camera, can take extra time when a special effect needs to be performed and captured flawlessly. (Well, not *flawlessly*, but you know... close enough for *MST3K*.)

- **PREPARING COPENHAGEN (TOP LEFT)**
  Reviewing the wooden standee of Copenhagen that Gypsy will destroy during one of the sketches in *Reptilicus*.

- **AUDIO MIXING (TOP CENTER)**
  We try to do as much of the audio mixing as possible during the shoot. Here, you get a look at the mixing board that our sound engineer sits at during production.

- **CAMERA SLATE (TOP RIGHT)**
  A quick look at the official slate that we used when shooting *The Return*. I shared directing responsibilities with the wonderful, and very funny, Rob Cohen.

- **TELEPROMPTERS (MIDDLE RIGHT)**
  Also, even though our cast know their lines, we have several teleprompters set up so that everyone – the actors, the crew and the puppet operators – can all stay on the same page... literally.

- **MONITORS (BOTTOM LEFT)**
  This shot gives you a nice sense of what it's like to be present on set, but always thinking about how things look on camera.

- **PROP PLACEMENT (BOTTOM CENTER)**
  It's a tough gig to be the host, emoting for the entire cast while performing elaborate visual gags. I always tried to check in with Jonah to make sure he was comfortable with all the tasks at hand. (He was.)

- **SCRIPT REVIEW (BOTTOM RIGHT)**
  Jonah and I talk over his motivation, while our wonderful head writer, Elliott Kalan, weighs in with the funny.

SHOOTING ON SET
Jonah Heston

One of the most important aspects of bringing back *MST*, of course, was finding the perfect test subject. I first met Jonah when I was a guest on the *Nerdist* podcast, where he was one of the hosts, and we just hit it off immediately. He was also a lifelong *MST* fan, with a really great, easy-going nature.

When it was time to select the next host, I felt like Jonah could be the perfect embodiment of where I imagined the show going. But you're probably thinking: *"That's all well and good, Joel, but this is the shooting section. What is Jonah like when he's on the set and making the show?"*

Well, for one thing, I've always been impressed with the amount of focus Jonah is able to maintain during a shoot, which involves long hours of

performing on camera, as well as even more hours rehearsing off-screen. The man works hard, and he also looks good while he's doing it. Which is important, because... well... he's on television!

Also, Jonah has a lot of experience as a standup comic, so he really got a lot of energy from having backers visit the set, which let him see their reactions and adjust his performance as he went.

So yeah, I guess what I'm trying to say is: Jonah Ray is an excellent, hard-working actor with great comic instincts, playing at the top of his game. And, just as important, he's up for anything. In fact, he's like Mary Poppins: "practically perfect in every way!"

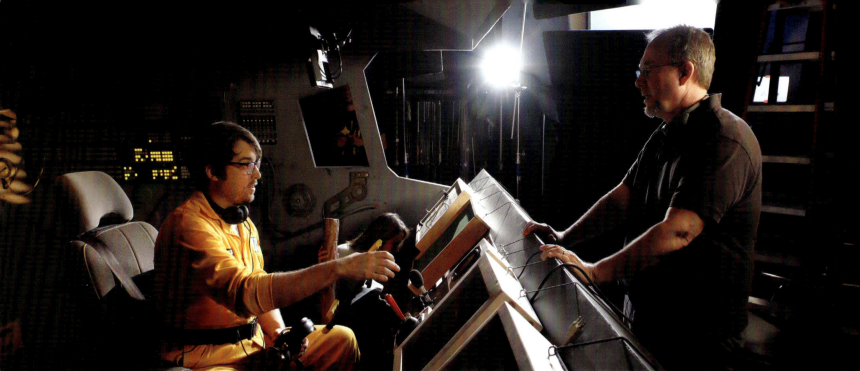

- **MIC'ED UP (TOP LEFT)**
Jonah wears a wire. For sound, of course. He'd never snitch.

- **NEED DIRECTIONS? (TOP RIGHT)**
Jonah, who is sitting at the console of the Backjack, talks shop with me... while I stand in outer space.

- **A REGULAR GUY (BOTTOM LEFT)**
Of course, the first thing I asked Jonah when I decided to offer him the job was, "Would you be okay with wearing a yellow jumpsuit?" He said... "Yes."

- **EVERY MONSTER (BOTTOM CENTER)**
The first sketch we shot with Jonah was actually the "Every Monster" rap, which was kind of a "trial by fire." Not only did he have to memorize and perform the complicated lyrics, but he also had to handle a crazy number of Seth's woodcut monsters. He managed to do both at the same time... and he made it look so easy!

- **GOOD IN COSTUME (BOTTOM RIGHT)**
One of the great things about Jonah is that he's willing to do whatever works best for a sketch. On *MST*, that involves wearing all kinds of kooky costumes. This was taken just before Jonah's "steampunk" sketch in *At The Earth's Core*.

SHOOTING ON SET
Robot Friends

Even with a wonderful host, a lot of the funny on *MST* also depends on having talented robot sidekicks. And while a lot of that talent has to come from the comic abilities of the actors, I also wanted to evolve the Bots' puppets a bit for *The Return*.

In the past, the puppets were a one-man job: talented comics like Josh Weinstein, Trace Beaulieu, Bill Corbett and Kevin Murphy performed the voices and operated the puppets at the same time. Over time, those guys became really talented puppeteers, even though none of them had puppeting experience when we started. But for *MST3K: The Return*, I wanted the Bots to be able to *do more*: handle props, make gestures, and give more "expressive" performances.

To do that, we first had to expand the Bot Trench (P.48) to accommodate more puppeteers, so there could be as many as three operators working in concert to animate a single bot, bunraku-style. And, at the same time, we also needed to make sure our cast could control Crow and Servo's mouths as they spoke their lines.

To get it all done, I asked our lead puppeteer, Grant Baciocco, to assemble a team. His first recruit was the wildly talented Russ Walko, who became our co-lead puppeteer, as well as our master puppet builder and technician. To round out the team, Grant also brought in the excellent Carla Rudy, Tim Blaney and Erik Kuska, while Russ set to work figuring out the new mechanical elements to expand the Bots' abilities.

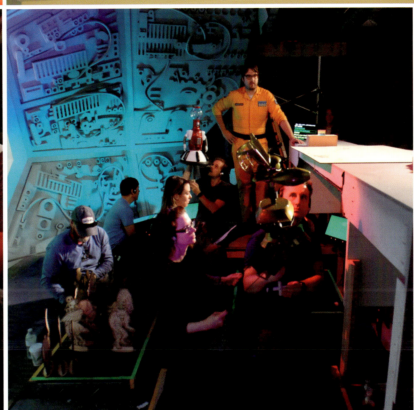

And then, of course, there were our actors. I told Jonah that the comics voicing Crow and Servo needed to be people he really respected and admired as performers and writers. They also needed to be good at improv, singing, impressions, and – most important – have great chemistry with Jonah.

I wanted him to have a team he felt like he could really "win" with. So when he suggested Baron Vaughn (Tom Servo) and Hampton Yount (Crow), and sent me links to some of their material on YouTube, I liked them right away. And, as you've seen, they've done an incredible job.

- **ROBOT VOICES (P.74, BOTTOM)**
Hampton, Baron and Rebecca were always just off-camera performing. For the new episodes, they were joined by M. Waverly (Grant Baciocco) and Growler (Russ Walko).

- **TRIGGER MEN (TOP LEFT)**
Hampton (*left*) and Baron (*right*) used special remote controls to move the bots' mouths in real time.

- **CROW LEGS (TOP CENTER)**
Puppeteers Tim Blaney and Russ Walko get Crow settled in a beanbag, where he can show off his new legs... which were a bit disturbing to see. (See P.14 for an early concept sketch.)

- **PUPPET MASTERS (BOTTOM LEFT)**
We had an incredible team of puppet operators behind the scenes. From left to right: Grant Baciocco, Tim Blaney, Erik Kuska, Carla Rudy, Russ Walko.

- **BEHIND THE DESK (BOTTOM CENTER)**
A unique perspective from behind the desk, where an entire team of puppeteers and prop-handlers ready themselves to perform "Every Monster."

- **GYPSY'S BODY! (BOTTOM RIGHT)**
Beez inspects her work – Gypsy and her "classy lady" soft sculpture body – while Caroline Louis positions the puppet version of a grand piano.

SHOOTING ON SET
Theater Silhouettes

Now, remember: even though the sketches take the most time to shoot, most of each episode of *MST* is actually spent riffing in the theater… which means we also needed to get the new silhouette sequences just right.

Back at Best Brains, in Eden Prarie, MN, we shot these scenes using a "luminance key." That might sound fancy, but it was actually just a wall of our studio, painted white.

For *The Return*, we upgraded to state-of-the-art greenscreen (*above left*), which let us create a much sharper composite image.

That was really important to me, because today's televisions are so big, and have such good picture, that it's important to make the riffing segments as clear as possible. Green-screen also let us create more elaborate and interactive visual gags, like when Servo floats up to hover over the screen (*top right*).

- **FULL BODY (BOTTOM LEFT)**
  To avoid appearing in the silhouette shots, our puppeteers had to wear these terrifying, bright green, full-body spandex suits.

- **MINI-GYPSY (BOTTOM RIGHT)**
  Tim Blaney, shown here capturing the silhouette for Gypsy's visit to the theater, is a veteran puppeteer. In fact, he's behind many classic film and television puppet performances, including Johnny Five from *Short Circuit* and Frank the Pug from *Men in Black*.

SHOOTING ON SET
Moonbase 13

Once we finished shooting all of the sketches on the Satellite of Love, the crew spent about a day moving all of the equipment and setting up in the opposite direction, so we could shoot all of the segments set on Moon 13.

As you can see in these pictures, this set was much larger and more involved than the SOL, with enough space to accommodate sketches (and weddings) in the middle, along with raised platforms on either side.

On the right, you can see the bandstand for "The Skeleton Crew" (more about them on P.79), while the platform set on the left was designed for Kinga and Max's as-yet-unrealized talk show, "Hot Cup of Kingachrome."

Originally, there *were* a few sketches where we were going to use the talk show set as an alternate location. But you know, once we got into production, we decided that we'd lose time moving all of the cameras and equipment to focus on the stage.

So, we agreed that it was better to keep the cameras in place, and shoot those scenes in the center aisle. Still, I'm glad the talk show set appears in the background of *The Return*, because I always imagined that as an "expansion," and something we can start to use more in the future. It also really helps you understand the scope of Kinga's ambitions for her liquid media empire.

SHOOTING ON SET
Kinga, Max & The Boneheads

I know that our past Mads have always had very dedicated followings (just like our past hosts and bots had), which meant that our new Mads had very big shoes to step into. Fortunately, for *The Return*, we were able to enlist the exceptional talents of Felicia Day (Kinga) and Patton Oswalt (Max), who were both fans of the original series themselves.

When you work with Felicia and Patton, one of the first things you realize is just that they're both total pros, as well as really strong intellects and character performers. One of the best things about that is that they both came to set with very clear ideas about who their characters were, which meant that I didn't need to do much to "embellish" their roles. Also, just as important, they seemed to "click" immediately, and just had wonderful comedic timing and flow together.

As for Rebecca Hanson (Synthia): when I first met her in Chicago, where she was a regular on the improv scene, I immediately thought about casting her as Synthia because of her strong resemblance to Mary Jo Pehl. But later, once I was able to focus on her voice, I also started to think of her as the new Gypsy. Back in the day, Josh and Trace were Mads, but also performed Tom Servo and Crow... so, I liked coming back to that idea, and having Rebecca play both Synthia *and* Gypsy.

- **READY FOR ACTION (TOP LEFT)**
  Felicia, with her amazing range of facial expressions, was a total pro, and willing to try just about anything to nail each sketch.

- **THE STEADY HAND (BOTTOM LEFT)**
  Co-director Rob Cohen hangs with Felicia and Patton as the crew preps the next shot in Moonbase 13.

- **BLUESCREEN (TOP CENTER)**
  A lot of Felicia and Patton's work was actually done in front of a blue-screen with a smaller crew, while the rest of the crew was shooting on the SOL. Studio time is expensive, so we needed to be able to prep and shoot two scenes at the same time when possible.

- **SOME REAL BONEHEADS (TOP RIGHT)**
  Like Synthia (aka Rebecca Hanson), our Boneheads, Tim Ryder (tall) and Zach Thompson (short) were regular fixtures on Chicago's reknowned improv circuit. Also, Tim happens to be married to Rebecca, which made life easier for them when they joined our live touring cast, since they got to do it together.

- **THE SKELETON CREW (BOTTOM RIGHT)**
  Our Bonehead Bandleader, Har Mar Superstar, behaves a bit like Cab Calloway as he leads The Skeleton Crew, a red-hot band of session performers in skeleton costumes. I was hoping to get a band that could actually play their instruments, and this one really did! (The day before. In a recording studio.) On set, they had to pantomime playing, like they were on *Top of the Pops!*

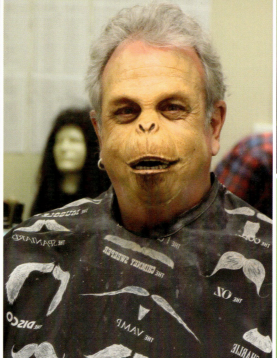

SHOOTING ON SET
Guest Stars

It was so much fun to invite some of the show's more famous friends to do cameos for Season 11. We felt it was something that might help us hype the Kickstarter to a broader audience, and it did seem to really help.

However, arranging the schedules and shoot times proved to be a real challenge. We needed to figure out a way to write the stories without requiring everyone to be on set in LA during such a condensed window of time.

So yeah, this is why each of our special guests ended up having their own spaceship! By using a greenscreen, we were able to shoot each celebrity when they were available, splitting the shoots between LA and NYC. And I gotta say, it worked very elegantly.

We shot almost all of our guests on set in LA. Then, after production ended, Ivan and I flew out to NYC to shoot with Jerry Seinfeld and Neil Patrick Harris.

- **OLD FRIENDS (LEFT)**
  One of the best parts of shooting the new season was the chance to bring back some familiar faces, like Kevin Murphy (Professor Bobo) and Bill Corbett (Observer).

- **CLASSIC MADS + NEW CAST! (BOTTOM RIGHT)**
  MST veterans Bill, Kevin and Mary Jo Pehl (Pearl Forrester) pose with Jonah, Hampton, Baron, Rebecca, and our incredible puppeteers.

- **GIZMONIC STAFF (P.80, TOP RIGHT)**
  We were so pleased that Wil Wheaton and Erin Gray agreed to appear as Gizmonic suits for our opening scene.

- **LARRY & VARNO (P.80, MIDDLE RIGHT)**
  Elliott Kalan's impression of *The Time Traveler's* Varno was so funny and weird we had to get him on camera to perform. I'm playing his ginger-headed savant, Larry.

- **PEARL & SYNTHIA (TOP LEFT)**
  When you get Mary Jo and Rebecca together, it's easy to see that Synthia is, in fact, a perfect clone of Pearl Forrester.

- **P.T. MINDSLAP (TOP RIGHT/BOTTOM LEFT)**
  Even I was a little bit starstruck when Mark Hamill agreed to cameo as Circus Impresario P.T. Mindslap. Even crazier: he came straight to set after shooting *The Last Jedi,* and shaved off his Skywalker beard for us!

- **FREAK MASTERSTROKE (BOTTOM CENTER)**
  My old pal Jerry Seinfeld gave me my first gig as a writer for his first stand-up special on HBO. During the Kickstarter, he was kind enough to promise he would make time for a cameo.

- **NEVILLE LeROY (BOTTOM CENTER)**
  Since I know Neil Patrick Harris through our shared love of stage magic, it was wonderful to have him do some on screen.

- **DOUG McCLURE (BOTTOM RIGHT)**
  We were very lucky to have the talented Joel McHale join us, both on set as Doug McClure and as a guest writer on *The Christmas That Almost Wasn't.* In case you're wondering, he was the only person on set as tall as Jonah Ray.

SEASON 12

The Gauntlet

Now that you've seen what's involved in **CONCEPTING**, **BUILDING** and **SHOOTING** a season of *Mystery Science Theater,* let's go through the process again while taking a look behind-the-scenes for *Season 12: The Gauntlet*!

In case you're wondering, the biggest difference between the two seasons – at least behind the scenes – was that Season 12 was a lot easier and faster to pull together than Season 11. That was mostly because this time around, we already had our sets and puppets built, and a cast and crew that were familiar with the entire process.

For a lot of reasons, focusing on a shorter season – just six episodes, instead of 14 – had real appeal for me. It meant that we'd be able to focus more time on fulfilling each individual epi-sode. On a creative level, managing the story arc for six episodes is simply more manageable.

Now it's your turn to see what happened... so turn the page and let's go!

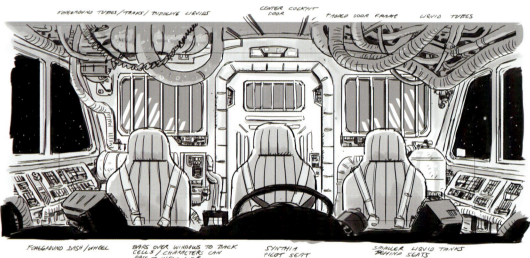

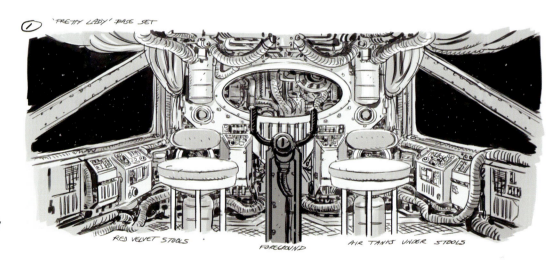

CONCEPT ART
Guy Davis

For the most part, we knew that Season 12 would be able to use all of the same sets that were designed for *The Return* in Season 11, but we also had a few new ideas we wanted to throw into the mix.

Once again, Guy Davis came through for us, offering wonderfully detailed renditions of three new vehicles, as well as a new location within Moonbase 13.

- **THE DEEP HURTING (LEFT)**
We knew that the season would end with Jonah, Synthia, and the Bots boarding a tour bus for Earth, to line up with our live tour, so we based the design on the actual tour bus for the *Watch Out for Snakes* live tour. The name – "The Deep Hurting" – was a sly reference to Ken Keasy and his Merry Pranksters' bus, named "Further."

- **THE PRETTY LADY (RIGHT)**
We created a space vehicle for Dr. Clayton Forrester and Frank (posthumously) called "The Pretty Lady," which was styled after Professor Evil and Max's vehicles in Blake Edwards' *The Great Race*. (Incidentally, Professor Evil and Max were the characters we styled Forrester and Frank after.) The name is based on a scream by Jerry Lewis.

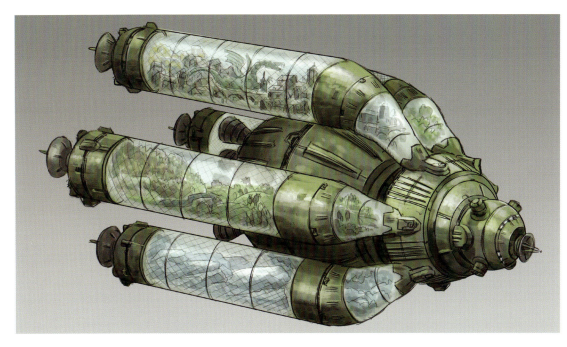

HIDDEN OVERHEAD LIGHT SOURCE   COBWEBS (MOON SPIDERS)

MST3K S12 / MOON 13 HALLWAY (DEC) / GUY DAVIS 2/26/18 REVISED   RUSTED METAL   OLD 50 GALLON DRUMS (CLEAR)   WWW.GUYDAVISARTWORKS.COM

- **THE ARK 3 (LEFT)**
  Dr. Donna St. Phibes' ship is a traveling animal sanctuary, with six unique environments to house B-movie monsters: arctic, desert, rain forest, urban, cave, and black and white. We couldn't call this vehicle "Earth 2" because of the made-for-TV movie from 1971, starring Marriette Hartley with two belly buttons.

- **MOON 13 DOOR SEQUENCE (RIGHT)**
  Some details for the Moonbase 13 doorway sequence that takes place during the startling conclusion to Season 12, as the Mads are shanghaied into their own theater.

CONCEPT ART
Seth Robinson

Once again, Seth Robinson produced a series of essential concept illustrations, including most of the new inventions, and a number of the more elaborate costume ideas we wanted to include.

One of the best things about Seth's work is that it creates a playful mood to suggest the fun of the sketch while being specific enough to be able to hand

to other members of the production team (props, hair, make-up, costumes, special effects) who can then execute finished work based on his drawings.

Seth's concept art was precise and specific enough that we were able to do just that: hand it straight to other members of the production team, who then knew exactly what to do with it.

Seth's Artwork

1. Time Machine Oven
2. Totino's Pizzaroll Cannon
3. Kinga & Max Puppet Drones
4. Hand Dryer Air Hockey
5. Fortune Meal
6. Air Dancer Pipe Organ
7. Gypsy's Grimace costume
8. Lady Bonehead uniform
9. Kingachrome Switcher
10. Waverly's Starling costume
11. Servo's razor octopus costume

PRODUCTION ART

Gary Glover

Last but not least, we also asked the multi-talented Gary Glover to help us out again, and he came through with more stunning work.

While Gary's work in Season 11 was mainly used for inspiration, some of his contributions for Season 12 actually appeared *on screen*, in the form of these startling 3-D background plates, which combined scratch-built models with lighting and particle effects in Photoshop. (Bet you didn't even realize those weren't real sets, huh?)

- **DEEP STORAGE (TOP LEFT)**
  The Kingachrome edition of *Pod People* stands waiting in the Moonbase 13 storage vault. Saving even the cheesiest of movies? The AFI should *be* this diligent.

- **THE AUDIO DRINK (BOTTOM LEFT)**
  This is the location on Moon 15 (the level beneath Moon 14) where all the leaked Kingachrome settles, and where Synthia, Ardy, and Bonesy find the liquified version of "Idiot Control Now."

- **BUBBULAT-R (RIGHT)**
  If you haven't gotten to read the *MST3K* comic book series, the Bubbulat-R is another Kingachrome technology that lets Kinga virtually drop Jonah and the Bots right into the pages of old comic books. For this image, Gary actually took the artwork that Todd Nauck created for the comics, built a model, photographed it, and then brought the elements into Adobe Creative Suite for finishing.

MODELS
Stoopid Buddy Stoodios

For models, we turned once again to our friends at Stoopid Buddy Stoodios, who did a remarkable job bringing Guy Davis' new concepts to life in vivid detail.

It's always so much fun to see how Stoopid Buddy's attention to the tiniest details turns cardboard, paper clips, and duct tape – combined with exquisite lighting – into a vivid on-screen world.

- **NEW SPACESHIPS (LEFT)**
  Here, the finished and painted models for "The Pretty Lady" (*top*), the "Ark 3" (*middle*), and "The Deep Hurting" (*bottom*).

- **MOON 13 DOORWAYS (BOTTOM RIGHT)**
  Lighting the flythrough models used to depict the doorway sequence on Moonbase 13 at the end of Episode 1206.

- **COCKPIT PLATES (TOP RIGHT)**
  To depict the cockpit of each ship, Stoopid Buddy created detailed background plates. We photographed each one before the studio shoot, so we were able to do a convincing job of compositing our actors into the space. To add a sense of realistic depth, we even created dashboard pieces (*top middle*). These were photographed separately and placed in front of the performer in post production.

(RE)BUILDING SETS
Satellite of Love & Moonbase 13

I've already gone into detail about our new sets (P.77), but the preparations for Season 12 reveal another important advantage that the newer sets have over the originals.

When we shot the original series, we had our own makeshift studio in Minnesota, so it didn't cost much to leave the sets assembled year-round. We never designed them to be broken down and re-assembled. When we were designing the updated Satellite of Love and Moonbase 13, we knew it would

be important to have sets that we could break down and put in storage in-between seasons, and set up again easily when it was time to shoot again. So, our new sets are more "modular" than before.

For Season 12, because of the size of the studio, we were also able to set the two main sets up side-by-side, rather than facing each other. This meant that "video village" could remain in one place throughout the shoot, and the walkways for the cast and

crew could stay the same. And, craft services were closer to the set, most importantly, because I like to snack.

Because Jonah, Tom, Crow, and Gypsy were going to be appearing on Moon 13 in Season 12, we decided to keep things more streamlined, and set up the main floor only, rather than the bandstand and talk show set. This was by design, since we thought the extra floor space would give the puppeteers more freedom to operate the Bots.

THEATER SEGMENTS

Recording the Riffing

Including Season 12 here also gives me a chance to share an interesting part of production that we didn't get to document in Season 11: the audio recording sessions where our cast perform their lines and riffs for the theater segments.

During Season 11, Jonah, Baron and Hampton were actually each isolated in their own recording booth, to keep their mics from picking up each others' lines. For Season 12, they suggested record-ing in the same booth, allowing them to better react to each other.

So here's the drill: our cast go into a recording booth together and record their lines while watching the movie. We all agree on our favorite takes, and move on. Meanwhile, in the control room, Elliott Kalan (our head writer) and I sit with sound engineer Tim Preston, giving input, suggestions, and – sometimes – last-minute riffs!

- **CONTROL ROOM (LEFT)**
  As we record the riffs for each movie, Elliott and I follow along with the scripts and make notes, especially when there are additions and edits.

- **IN THE BOOTH (RIGHT)**
  Our cast recorded riffs while watching the movies *and* paying close attention to the script. As you can see on the monitor, we've already added the silhouette seats to ensure that no-one riffs on visuals that might be covered up later in the process.

THEATER SEGMENTS
Shooting Silhouettes

Once the riffs are recorded, we have everything we need to shoot our silhouette sequences in front of the green screen. The theater seats are added in post.

If you compare this shoot to the silhouette shoot from Season 11 (P.76), you'll see that we made the footprint of the platform smaller to allow more room for the puppeteers around Jonah. This was especially helpful when we staged some of the more elaborate production numbers and visual gags, like the Crowrahnas that appear during *Killer Fish*.

- **THE BIG PICTURE (LEFT)**
  Jonah – in a black "silhouette" jumpsuit that won't reflect the green screen – sits on a platform, as the puppeteering team operate Crow and Tom Servo from below. While the riff audio plays out loud, a teleprompter follows along in the script, and a second monitor lets them see the silhouettes composited on top of the movie in real-time, helping them sync their performance with the picture and audio.

- **SILHOUETTE GAGS (TOP RIGHT)**
  The puppeteering team and I with additional Crowrahna puppets. We planned to have a Crowrahna chorus line during "Below the Dam," but it got cut in post.

- **IT TAKES A TEAM (BOTTOM RIGHT)**
  The green screen team (*clockwise*): Jonah, Russ Walko, Erik Kuska, Tim Blaney, Carla Rudy and Grant Baciocco.

SHOOTING ON SET
Back
In Orbit

Being back on set was really a pleasure, especially since things felt noticeably calmer... and with good reason. We were better prepared the second time around. We were lucky enough to have most of our original crew from Season 11 return, so everyone already knew what to expect, and had a good idea of how everything would work.

Also, with fewer episodes this season, we decided to keep the focus of *The Gauntlet* with our main cast, and bring in fewer guests than we did in *The Return*. However, we *did* get the chance to bring back Josh Weinstein to reprise his role as one of the original Mads, Dr. Laurence Erhardt.

We also introduced a few new recurring characters: Deanna Rooney came on board as both Dr. Donna St. Phibes, the Jane Goodall of B-movie monsters, and as our first "Lady Bonehead," and producer Ivan Askwith lent us his deep, melodic voice as Ardy's new talking dog, Bonesy.

Truth be told, Bonesy is based on my dog Jonesy, and Ivan Askwith, our producer and Kickstarter guru. I was so grateful to Ivan for his vision and expertise when we did the Kickstarter campaign that I decided to offer him a role in the show if he wanted it. I was thrilled he was up for it, and because of his performance, I feel Bonesy is a very memorable character.

- **DR. ERHARDT! (TOP, CENTER LEFT)**
It was so great having Josh back on set with us. Josh and I first met when he was a teenager and have been friends ever since. Back in the early days of *Mystery Science Theater*, Josh was always our most solid joke writer; I trust his ability implicitly. So when I forwarded him the script, I told him to add whatever jokes he wanted, and that's what we went with.

- **DR. ST PHIBES (TOP, CENTER RIGHT)**
Deanna is an incredibly capable performer, so I deliberately gave her an element that would be a challenge for most actors: operating the Lady of the Deep puppet. This required her to perform two characters at the same time – a little bit like a ventriloquist with a dummy. I am happy to report, she *and* the Lady of the Deep puppet did a very convincing job.

- **A NEW DIRECTOR (BOTTOM CENTER)**
For *The Gauntlet*, I was able to enlist one of my favorite directors, Rob Schrab, to run the room during our sketch segments. Rob has this great energy that's both manic and affable at the same time. He also has a great eye, and a killer sense of humor.

- **BONEHEAD TRIO (BOTTOM RIGHT)**
When she wasn't performing as St. Phibes, Deanna also joined Kinga's minions as our first Lady Bonehead. I'm looking forward to seeing how cosplayers evolve the look!

- **WHEN WORLDS COLLIDE (TOP LEFT)**
  One of our creative ambitions for *The Gauntlet* was to have Jonah, Tom and Crow invade Moonbase 13. It seemed like a nice change of pace to have them run amok in Kinga and Max's lair, so we embraced the challenge of letting the Bots interact with our cast on an open set, without the convenience of the Bot Trench.

- **PUTTIN' ON THE RITZ (TOP RIGHT)**
  Sometimes, when we're shooting song numbers, they can take on a life of their own. For one of Season 12's most ambitious songs ("Concepts"), we realized it was a bit like something Professor Harold Hill would sing in *The Music Man,* which was the inspiration for Kinga and Max's hats. It's one of those fun moments we used to do in the old show, cutting back to Moon 13 to see how the Mads are reacting to Jonah and the Bots.

- **ARDY & BONESY (BOTTOM LEFT)**
  Here, Russ Walko animates Bonesy, a puppet he fabricated. On the set, there was lots of speculation as to what breed Bonesy is, because his face and body are obscured by his spacesuit. But I'm here to tell you, Bonesy is an Old English bulldog.

- **CONTAINMENT 2.0 (BOTTOM RIGHT)**
  Here, Kinga and Max shoot their final scene with the Containment Vessel, which is what we call the unit that holds the Kingachrome waste created after each experiment. It's like those containers that hold spent fuel rods in power plants, but maybe even more toxic. For *The Gauntlet,* we added slots for 6 more movies, and also put steps for Kinga and Max to stand on, so that – SPOILERS! – it can trap them in their own theater in the finale.

- **HANGING BACKSTAGE (LEFT)**
Deanna (Dr. Donna St. Phibes), Baron (Tom Servo), and Hampton (Crow) have some good-natured fun hanging out in the production offices while the rest of us are preparing the studio for the next scenes.

- **OPERATING PROCEDURE (TOP CENTER)**
Even though Felicia is a total pro, I was a little bit concerned when it was time for her to shoot our Totino's Pizza Roll Cannon at Patton. (After all, it's a well-known fact that his face is insured with Lloyd's of London!) So, I wanted to make sure she knew how to handle the cannon when the safety was off.

(By the way, this was actually a standard issue t-shirt cannon, retrofitted to handle foam rubber pizza roll rounds. And yes: We tested it with real pizza rolls, but it was a huge mess. A huge, delicious mess.)

- **PHONEHEAD (TOP RIGHT)**
One of our veteran Boneheads, Zach Thompson, checks his phone during a break between takes on Moonbase 13.

- **LAST LOOKS (BOTTOM RIGHT)**
Every season, we try to give all of our crew members – and visiting Kickstarter backers! – a chance to take photos behind the desk on the Satellite of Love. When we wrapped up *The Gauntlet*, I made sure to get one with Jonah, co-director Rob Schrab, Hampton and Baron.

SHOOTING ON SET
Prop Masters

Before we wrap things up, there's one last aspect that's kind of interesting to show you about how *MST* works behind the scenes.

As you know, a lot of our sketches – especially the Invention Exchange – feaure elaborate visual gags, or involve Crow and Tom Servo interacting with complex props.

What you might not know is how much work and creativity goes into designing those props to make sure they work just right on screen.

- **ENDLESS WINE (TOP ROW)**
  During one sketch in *Atlantic Rim*, Crow and Tom Servo instruct Jonah to pour out some wine for everyone who died in the movie... and then tell him keep pouring until they say "when" (*left*). Like a clown car, we wanted to show an impossible amount of wine coming out of the bottle, so our team designed a tubing system that let the crew pump wine up into the bottle, which then emptied into a bucket below the counter (*right*).

- **HAND DRYER AIR HOCKEY (BOTTOM ROW)**
  For the Invention Exchange in *Lords of the Deep*, Jonah and the Bots introduce an air hockey table powered by a bathroom hand dryer (*left*). We just had to test whether we could actually use the hand dryer to power an air hockey table. Sadly, it didn't work... but we solved the design challenge with sound effects and a layer of WD-40 on the puck.

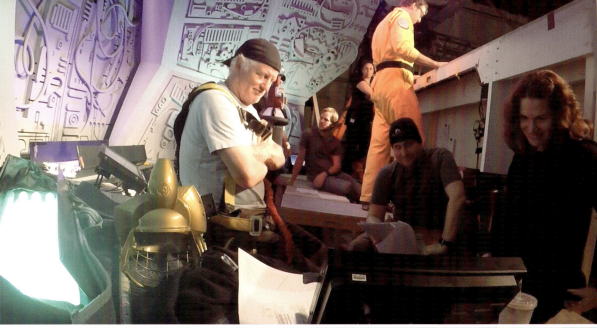

SHOOTING ON SET

Puppet Masters

- **BEHIND THE SCENE (TOP LEFT)**
  A rare view from directly behind the desk. On the left, Russ is operating Tom Servo, and on the right, Grant is puppeting Crow. The monitors are there with the camera feed reversed, so they can see how the bots look on screen, and the scripts are hanging just above so they can track any stage directions the writers include in the script.

- **CHECKING THE SHOT (TOP RIGHT)**
  Puppeteers Tim Blaney and Carla Rudy watch as we replay the previous performance. Even if I like a particular take, I prefer to make sure the puppeteers are also happy with it.

- **PUPPETS FROM ABOVE (BOTTOM LEFT)**
  Carla and Tim share a laugh between takes with the Kinga and Max marionette drones, while standing on the scaffolding directly above the set. This is also where Tim stands to puppet Gypsy throughout the season. (You can see Gypsy hanging out in the background, waiting for her next shot.)

- **PUPPETS FROM BELOW (BOTTOM RIGHT)**
  To let Crow and Servo move freely through Moon 13, Grant, Carla, and Russ sat on rolling platforms (we call them crawlers) on the ground, just below the camera frame. I have to admit, without our desk and bot trench, these photos look very Muppet-y to me.

Acknowledgeme

nts

This might be the hardest part of the book to write, because there have been so many people who just did amazing work to help #BringBackMST3K.

We can't begin to give each of those people the credit and thanks they deserve, so I hope that every now and then, when you rewatch these seasons, you'll also take a minute to watch the credits at the end of each episode, and think about how many people were really working at the top of their game to help bring you these new episodes. After all, if you were a backer, you basically bankrolled all of these people!

Alternaversal Vision Team

The **ALTERNAVERSAL VISION TEAM** was the first group I was able to form and hire on a full-time basis. I call them the Vision Team because we are, together, the vanguard when it comes to the process of anticipating, fulfilling, and maintaining all *MST3K* creative projects.

Also, the entire team writes for the show, as well as the comic books, the live tour, and any other new projects.

I first met Seth, Matt and Mary a few years before the Kickstarter, when I was teaching a riff writing workshop at Bucks County Community College. All three of them had very unique spirits, exuded creativity, and were talented writers. After the class, I asked them to write on some experimental projects, and also my one man show. They were fun, great to work with, and among my first choices to start the creative team at Alternaversal.

JOEL HODGSON, well... you already know me. About 30 years ago, I created *Mystery Science Theater 3000,* and for the first hundred shows, I was the host. These days, I tend to try to visualize the big picture, and work with the Vision Team to figure out how to make it all happen.

HAROLD BUCHHOLZ is the President of Alternaversal, and an Executive Producer on *MST3K*. He manages all of our business concerns, including budgets and resources. We first met when Harold approached me about creating a comic book version of *Cinematic Titanic,* and he was really the one who first convinced me on the whole idea of using Kickstarter to bring back *MST3K*.

SHARYL VOLPE is our wonderful Operations Manager, and an Associate Producer on *MST3K*. She supervises meetings and communication, as well as project planning. We first met when our sons were on the same Little League team, and I learned she had a lot of experience with writing and operations. She also had this very cool aesthetic that I hoped would rub off on the rest of us.

SETH ROBINSON is an Associate Producer on the series, and a creative producer for the *MST3K* brand. As you've seen, he's also a talented artist who helped shape the look of the new episodes (P.26, P.86). Seth oversees the visual elements for the series, live tour, merch and comic.

MATT MCGINNIS is an Associate Producer on the series, and coordinates pre-visualization, sound fulfillment, and post-production for the new seasons of *MST*. He also supervised fulfillment of our comic book series for Dark Horse.

MARY ROBINSON is our lead writer and has written on nearly every episode of the Netflix series, our live shows and the comic books. Before working on *MST3K*, Mary was working as a Montessori teacher, which I thought would bring some new perspective to the show and the writing process.

Creative Collaborators

While our Vision Team really got everything *started*, a show like *Mystery Science Theater* requires the hard work and talent of many more people. There's not enough room to tell you about *everyone* who made essential contributions to the new seasons, but on these final pages, I want to introduce you to some more of the people who helped bring these new seasons of *MST3K* to life.

ELLIOTT KALAN, our incredible Head Writer, has the very difficult job of figuring out how to take all of the ideas we want to include, and making them work as a unified whole. We count on Elliott to make sure we have a consistent story arc that is charming, funny, and a good read. He's also really fun to work with, and he's much more positive than you'd expect for someone this funny.

PAUL & STORM, who wrote most of the songs for the new episodes, and were also writers and producers on, have been my go-to guys for clever, funny music for a long time. I don't think I can pick just one favorite from the songs they wrote for *MST3K*, but I really think the "Every Country (Has A Monster)" rap from *The Return*, and "Get In Your Mech and Drive" from *The Gauntlet,* are just incredible.

BOBBY LOPEZ, who contributed some featured songs for *The Return*, has got to be the only EGOT winner who has ever worked on *MST3K*. We worked out his songs over Skype, and I have to tell you, he's probably a musical genius. Watching him come up with songs on the other side of the screen was like seeing Einstein work out a theory at a blackboard. I'm grateful that he was able to find time in his schedule while working on a little movie called *Frozen 2*.

IVAN ASKWITH, our producer, was responsible for leading the entire Kickstarter process, from our first videos and updates, to our rewards and special events, through production, and even developing and curating this book. Ivan has an uncanny ability to anticipate what almost 50,000 backers want and need, and really cared about making everyone happy. We couldn't have done this without him.

ROB COHEN, my co-director for *The Return*, is someone I've known for a long, long time, but we didn't work together until I was on Paul Feig's *Other Space*. Having Rob co-direct the sketches was one of the most important choices we made for Season 11. Watching him direct, I just couldn't get over how good he is. He tunes in so well with each performer, and can really speak to each of them in their own language.

ROB SCHRAB was my co-director for *The Gauntlet*. He was just as incredible to work with, which just proves that many of the best comedic directors are named Rob. Rob is so good at running the room, and seeing where all the actors are with their performances, that I can take a step back, keep an eye on the in-camera effects and puppets, and make sure it all looks right on camera. He's also just an incredibly fun, and funny, guy to be around.

JONATHAN STERN is one of our Executive Producers, and also the founder and leader of Abominable Pictures, our main production partner. I first met Jon on Paul Feig's *Other Space,* and just knew right away that his team was the best I'd ever seen. He's great at working with creatives, totally undaunted by production issues, and really seems to care about the work. He also put together an *amazing* team for us.

SHOUT! FACTORY was our first real partner in bringing back *Mystery Science Theater 3000*, and its founders – Garson Foos, Richard Foos and Bob Emmer (*clockwise from top left*) – were with us every step of the way. "The Trio," as we call them, got the rights we needed to make more episodes of the show. Also, by selling the classic episodes on DVD over the years, Shout! Factory really helped keep *MST3K* alive in people's minds until we could bring the show back.

FRANNY BALDWIN & DAVE SOLDINGER are our fearless producers. One of the biggest benefits of working with a top-flight crew like Abominable is that you get access to this kind of expertise. Franny and "Super Dave", as we call him, are responsible for problem solving, managing the crew, supervising the budget, and making sure we get through post-production.

SAMANTHA KUESTER is our Costume Designer, and we were really fortunate to get her for the show. When you work with garments and costumes, you really need to be a great people person, and a careful observer. Samantha also really understands how to use costumes to reinforce and amplify our characters, which I feel is essential to our storytelling.

LESLEY KINZEL was an Associate Producer on *The Return*, a writer on both seasons, and a valuable consultant to our Kickstarter team. As a long-time fan of *Mystery Science Theater* and a journalist, Lesley really helped us understand what *MST* means to many of the fans, and helped advocate for what she thought the fan community would care about most in the updated show.

CAROLINE LOUIS is our Prop Master, which can be an especially hard job on a show like *MST3K*, where we're shooting everything "live" in-camera. This means Caroline is responsible for coordinating a ton of props and having each one waiting at exactly the right time so that production goes smoothly.

RUSS WALKO is our Lead Puppet Fabricator and Co-Lead Puppeteer, operates Tom Servo, and is such an important part of the new *Mystery Science Theater*. As a longtime veteran of Jim Henson's Creature Shop, Russ understands puppets and their unique physics in a profound way. It was great to collaborate with him. I trusted him to deliver really great looking and mechanically sound props and puppets, and he always came through.

MIKE MURNANE, our Lead Model Builder, has this unique style that involves making anything and everything out of cardboard. When we first met with Stoopid Buddy, they sent us Mike's work and suggested that his style would be great for a lot of background elements. We told them we wanted to do the whole *show* that way! I depended on Mike to supervise the builds on all the models and give them warmth and charm.

GRANT BACIOCCO is our Co-Lead Puppeteer, operates Crow, and is just an incredibly talented, versatile and funny performer. I've actually known Grant since he worked on *Cinematic Titanic* about 15 years ago, and first asked him to help out with *Mystery Science Theater* when we started shooting new introduction segments with Crow and Servo for our annual Turkey Day Marathon. There are many wonderful things I could say about Grant, but what stands out most is his genuine, warm enthusiasm.

AARON SOMERS and his team were key collaborators, and we were really lucky to find him. His team has a workshop in Brooklyn, which let us visit and be hands-on during the very important construction of the Satellite of Love, a multitude of props for Season 11, and set pieces like Kinga's Ziggurat, the Containment Vessel, and the God Monitor.

BEEZ MCKEEVER, our Robot Costumer, is a veteran of the original *MST*, and – to me – the living embodiment of the creative scene in Minneapolis. She made a big impression on the *Mystery Science Theater* aesthetic over the years, and I was so excited to invite her to join the new show. Almost every robot costume and accessory we use needs to be custom-made, and Beez is ingenious at making it all work. It also helps that she is very familiar with Tom and Crow's measurements.

JUSTIN LIEB & RYAN MARTIN, our Abominable Production Designers (for *The Return* and *The Gauntlet*, respectively), worked with the rest of the LA crew to make sure the Moon 13 and Backjack interior sets came together and looked just right. And, as their photo illustrates, they were also really fun to work with.

ACKNOWLEDGEMENTS
Revival League

So, yeah... I guess that brings us to the end of the book, which is really also – for many us – the end of our work on these past two seasons of *Mystery Science Theater 3000*, and the entire Kickstarter, and the campaign to #BringBackMST3K.

We've said this a lot of times over the past three years, but it's still important, so on behalf of everyone who worked on *The Return* and *The Gauntlet,* I want to say it again:

Thank you to all of our Kickstarter backers, and to everyone who joined us for the Season 12 Pledge Drive, for making everything you see in this book possible. We're so grateful for your trust, and for your support, that lets us continue to return to the world of *Mystery Science Theater.*

Also, while we don't have enough room in this book to list each of our 48,270 generous backers, I really wanted to include as many as possible... and since this book is all about life behind-the-scenes, I thought we could at least share pictures of some of the groups of backers who came to visit the set during production, and to appear as Observers during Kinga's wedding in the final episode of *The Return.*

Wedding Observers

Patricia Adams
Mike Aronow
Kyle Bacon
Jordan Brown
Andrew Brunner
Nick Carlson
John Cookson
Jason D'Itri
Larry Dunn
Zachary Forsyth

Tony Goggin
Dave Goldblatt
Spencer Goldrich
Ike Haldan
Jason Harder
Larry Hastings
Jeff Hill
Adam King
Darcy Madi
Guillermo Martinez

Juan Martinez
Colin McRavey
Drew Minoff
Amber Oliver
Paul Reynolds
Kathryn Rice
Joe Sherman
Ben Tobin

Production Set Visitors

Eric Albertson
John Allison
David Bacon
David Cruise
Meredith Cooper
Jeri Ellsworth
Stuart Ferguson
Matt Giles
Isabel Gorbach
Jonathan Gorbach

Laura Gorbach
Jim Hicks
Steve Jablonsky
Karen Kaske
Steven Landberg
Chris Lundin
Shane Matheson
Jason McGrody
Tom Medved
Dan Milano

Matthew Mills
Tom O'Keefe
Crystal O'Keefe
Paul Rabogliatti
Erik Schmollinger
Christa Starr
Philip Stephens
David Sublette
Tami Sublette

Photos

Ivan Askwith
Grant Baciocco
Harold Buchholz
Joel Hodgson
Lesley Kinzel
Darren Michaels
Michael Ribas
Seth Robinson
Karrie Stouffer
Shout! Factory
Stoopid Buddy

Artwork

Crist Ballast
Brett "2D" Bean
Marty Baumann
Guy Davis
Andrew Dickman
Ray Frenden
Gary Glover
Josh Pruett
Seth Robinson
Steven Sugar

Executive Producers

Mike Aronow
Tom Gates
Larry Hastings
John Lyons
Dan Lanigan
Richard Parrish
Amelia Kane Shannon
Greg Tally

Special Thanks

Leslie Anderson
Fred Bimbler
Lindsay Bowen
Evan Brown
Jack Brungardt
Robert Bukoski
John Carney
Chris Chang
Adam & Andy Cruz
Jonathan Coulton
Sarah J. De Bruin

Derek Delgaudio
Karlee Esmailli
Jordan Fields
Vanessa Keiko Flanders
Dana Gould
Adam Hann-Byrd
Trish Hadley
Dan Harmon
John Hodgman
Penn & Teller
John Krasno

Vanessa Lauren
Bobby Lopez
Nancy Ly
Alexandra Marvar
Jordan McArthur
Dave McIntosh
Kate Micucci
Barry Munden
Todd Nauck
Nathan Palmer
Christian Pearson

Michael Ribas
Justin Roiland
Vinny Rutherford
Dana Snyder
Michael Stewart
Karrie Stouffer
Yancey Strickler
Randy Stradley
Ken Swezey
Larry Tanz
Samantha Tinsley

Steve Vance
Pendleton Ward
Dylan Werner
Liz Wiltsie
Rob Zabreckie
CrowdOx
Dark Horse Comics
Kickstarter
Meltdown Comics
Netflix
Vimeo & VHX